# *Free Money*

## Plan for Prosperity

Rodger Malcolm Mitchell

 Published by PGM Worldwide, Inc., 921 Pontiac Road, Wilmette, IL 60091. First Edition. 47K words.

**Library of Congress Cataloging in Publication Data**
Mitchell, Rodger Malcolm
*FREE MONEY:* A discussion of common economic beliefs, showing why they are wrong, and what actions America can take to assure its economic prosperity/ Rodger Malcolm Mitchell

ISBN 978-0-9658323-1-1

**Attention: Colleges and universities, corporations and professional organizations.** Quantity discounts on bulk purchases are available. Please contact the publisher.

*For Phyllis*
*Thank God for Phyllis*

# *Table of Contents*

## *Preface*

The first version of this book, published in 1997, was titled, "The Ultimate America." It was re-titled and edited in 2001. The version you are reading was re-edited in 2005, but maintains the conclusions and predictions of the earlier books – with one major exception: In a 1993 speech, I proposed to economists at the University of Missouri, Kansas City, that all federal borrowing should be eliminated.

Subsequently, historical research by Professors Joelle Leclaire (Buffalo State College) and Corinne Pastoret (University of Burgundy, Dijon) has supported that notion.

I am gratified that eight years after the first version was published, its comments about our economy have proved prescient. In 1997, the Chicago Tribune newspaper published an editorial headlined, *"Clinton, GOP hail budget, tax deal . . . would yield the first balanced budget since 1969"* Chicago Tribune, *May 3, 1997.*"

I predicted this much-applauded act would cause a recession if we were lucky and a depression if we were not. We were lucky. We had the recession.

If we were not so lucky, and the surplus had lasted longer, this is what might have happened:

1817-1821: Federal debt reduced 29%. Depression began 1819.
1823-1836: Federal debt reduced 99%. Depression began 1837.
1852-1857: Federal debt reduced 59%. Depression began 1857.
1867-1873. Federal debt reduced 27%. Depression began 1873.
1880-1893: Federal debt reduced 57%. Depression began 1893.
1920-1930: Federal debt reduced 36%. Depression began 1929.

Those who hailed the disastrous budget tax deal, continue to call for a balanced budget. If they succeed, we again will have a recession or a depression, and if history is a guide, the same politicians and economists will have learned nothing.

Not that all economists are confused. I met some who have learned from history. On November 17, 2003, when I spoke at the Center for Full Employment, the University of Missouri, Kansas City (posted at http://www.rodgermitchell.com/resources/html), I met economists who understand that the budget deficit not only doesn't threaten us, but actually is necessary, though in a different form.

Now that research has been completed, supporting the fundamental theories in Free Money, I hope, with the imprimatur of academia, the Free Money theory may gain the following that logic and history have not provided.

## *Introduction -- Skepticism, And the Voice of Mother*

*"A growing economy must have a growing supply of money. Where will we find the money to grow our economy?"*

My daughters, Leslie and Julia, grown and with children, always have idolized my wife, Phyllis. They laugh about their childhood, when their mother would caution them not to do something or another. She would end each warning with a forecast of a misfortune that would befall them if they disobeyed. "Don't go to school without your boots. It'll rain and you'll get your feet wet and catch cold."

They sometimes would tempt fate. (After all, it wasn't raining yet, and who wants to wear boots?) They would go without boots, and of course it did rain. And of course, they caught colds.

My wife's ability to understand the present and to see the future was given the name, "The Voice of Mother." My daughters learned not to ignore "The Voice of Mother." My wife earned her respect through her knowledge, her experience and her ability to analyze the empirical data of life. She sees reality.

Our economy lacks a "Voice of Mother." Economists, politicians and the media agree that:

> *"We can't afford the debt we have. It means there is no capital for anybody to borrow, and just the interest on the debt is eating us alive."*

So said Representative Louise Slaughter in 1993, in the midst of a powerful, economic expansion. Rep. Slaughter was neither first nor last to declare horror at the size of the federal debt and to predict its terrible, imminent repercussions. She was neither first nor last to ignore the reality of the world around her.

In 1947, the federal debt totaled $250 billion. By 1980, it had grown to $900 billion, exceeding a threefold increase in just thirty-three years.

As shocking as that debt increase may have seemed to some, it scarcely compared to what followed. In the sixteen-year period from 1980 to 1996, the federal debt grew sixfold. If ever there were a test of Representative Slaughter's philosophy, this was it. We were presented, not with theory, but with a scientific experiment, a massive, unprecedented explosion of federal debt.

Catastrophe was at hand. "Voodoo economics" (a.k.a. "Reaganomics") had the nation poised at the abyss. We were about to plunge into bankruptcy or worse.

Experts told us something remarkable was about to happen. And they were right. We continued our remarkable economic growth combined with low unemployment, low inflation and a powerful bull stock market. The economy hardly could have been better.

Yet today, attitudes about federal debt have not changed, as Congress again wishes to drag us from a deficit into a federal surplus.

The experts act like stubborn weather forecasters. Each day they predict zero for tomorrow, only to see temperatures soar to the eighties. Undeterred, they continue to forecast zero.

**What Is "Cognitive Dissonance" And How Does It Relate to the Federal Debt?**

Why do educated people ignore empirical evidence? They suffer from the human trait psychologists call, "cognitive dissonance." It is the ability to adopt, then to embrace, then to defend with passion, two mutually exclusive ideas.

Religion can provide examples of cognitive dissonance. We pray and our prayers are answered. We pray again and again, but nothing happens. Despite the failures, which in number may outweigh the successes, our belief in prayer never ends. Cognitive dissonance.

The beliefs of experts affect our own beliefs. You may have adopted some. Why would you not, given the reinforcement of our leaders and the media?

This book may attempt the impossible. It will ask you to examine your convictions. It will challenge you to change those convictions.

None of us were born with convictions. Nor did we develop most of our opinions through research. We were taught by those who "know." They injected us with the opinions of experts.

Do you believe a scientist sets out with a clean mental slate? Do you think he or she finds evidence, makes observations, runs experiments, and after eliminating alternatives, builds a theory and system of belief?

This is the logical way, but it is not the human way, nor generally the scientific way. Often the process works in reverse. Theory and belief may come before observation. Evidence is gathered to support the theory. Experimental results are rejected if they disagree with the preconceived notion.

That has been the fate of economics.

**The Messenger Is Not the Message**

We are charmed by authority. Put "PhD" or "MD" after a name and that person's words become Truth. Yet, every year, MD's write false diet books and PhDs put forth one more theory of cosmic evolution, each of which is disputed by other PhDs.

Medical doctors told us polio came from swimming. And hair loss could be prevented by massage. And vitamin C could, then could not, then again could, prevent colds. What is it now? I can't recall.

PhDs tell us dinosaurs were cold blooded or warm blooded, or both. Birds or non-birds. Made extinct by disease. Or by volcanos. Or by meteors.

Professors of economics gave us the Great Depression.

Authority fathers repetition. Repetition creates credibility. Credibility echoed, produces believability. Believability evolves to proof, and proof masquerades as fact.

Economics analyzes past micro-events to predict the future. But these micro-events describe only a tiny fraction of the past and may not be representative. And the future never duplicates the past, which makes proof inconvenient.

Economic theories are filled with *selected* data, any obscure piece of which can be used as proof. With selected data one can "prove" the Great Depression was a time of prosperity, or never happened. Different selected data are used endlessly to show why the Depression came and went. Every economist has a slightly different theory.

In 1798 economist Thomas Malthus "proved" that population growth always outruns production growth, so humankind must end in poverty. This continued to be Truth into the 1950's.

After two hundred years preparing for the apocalypse, economists admit that poverty is caused by many factors. Most are social and political. None are related to our ability to produce, which today exceeds our consumption needs by more than ever.

Malthus's theory was defended by PhD's, despite a lack of evidence and despite the annoying failure of the human race to die.

Some people *continue* to believe Malthus. Such is the persistence of belief and cognitive dissonance. Malthus, and most experts, are worshiped more for prominence than for accuracy.

Karl Marx and Friedrich Engles wrote *The Communist Manifesto* and *Das Kapital.* They predicted the success of communism. The laggard economies of Russia, China, North Korea and Cuba testify otherwise. Yet, millions continue to believe in this economic self-mutilation. More cognitive dissonance.

Socialism began well before Marx. Plato discussed it twenty centuries ago in *The Republic.* Sir Thomas More endorsed it in his sixteenth century *Utopia*. With so much time to study socialism, we now should know everything about it and all questions should be answered. Yet we seem no closer to agreement on this subject than we are on most other economic questions.

Recently I heard two people argue about welfare. One said, "It breeds indolence." The other said, "We can't let poor people starve." My thought was, "After two thousand years of debate, is this as far as we've come? The same arguments? The same responses? What science but economics would allow two thousand years of experience to pass without a single step toward settling a basic issue?"

*Economics is a religion.*

Economics is not like other sciences. It more closely resembles religion, in which authority is more important than evidence. Economists explain their inaccurate predictions the way cult leaders explain God's failure to protect the innocent or the world's failure to end. They do not change their theories. They tack on ancillary theories that explain why their original theories failed, yet remain valid.

I have belittled the experts for one reason: to make you dubious about all economic theories -- including mine. You won't accept an idea, just because it is in print. Don't reject an idea, just because it disagrees with your preconceived notions. Think about the evidence and the logic, then decide.

Because economics offers so much data and so many theories, the lay person may feel only a learned professor from a prestigious school can make sense of it. Yet there are fundamentals every lay person can understand.

Weather forecasting is equally complex and filled with data. Yet, you needn't be a meteorologist to understand why winter is cold and summer is warm.

When you look at the fundamentals, you will realize, the messenger is not the message.

**Feel the Knees of Infants.**

What would you say if I told you, infants have no kneecaps? It's true of some, who have cartilage, not yet ossified. Did you dismiss my comment, because I am not an MD? Or, would you like to see evidence before deciding? The best way to know if I'm right or wrong is to feel the knees of infants. Empirical evidence.

Don't accept or doubt my words. Don't accept the words of the academics, the politicians or the media. Look at the empirical evidence. Feel the knees of infants.

**What Are the "Stop and Think" Boxes?**

You will find sprinkled through this book, small sections labeled "**Stop and Think.**" I cannot ask you to analyze your beliefs, if I conduct a one-way communication. You must participate. You must learn not only by reading, but by mentally doing. Your belief must come from your own effort and logic.

Albert Einstein and other physicists engaged in the same process with their thought problems -- exercises in pure reason. **"Stop and Think"** is the economics' equivalent of thought problems in physics.

**Stop and Think:** Imagine circumstances in which authority and/or conventional wisdom later were proven wrong. Do not limit yourself to economics.

Think about medicine and nutrition. What former Truths have been proven wrong? Think about psychology. Think about the financial markets, politics, war. Think about Prohibition, welfare and the war on drugs. Think about things your parents told you. What elements did these beliefs have in common? Write your ideas and save your paper in a file labeled "Stop and Think."

**What is "Free Money"?**

Money is made from nothing and is backed by nothing. It has no intrinsic value and no stated value. It exists as a vague promise:

To the U.S. government, money is free. The government can produce unlimited quantities at a moment's notice and without cost. Those three factors – no limit, no time and no cost – make money perhaps the least costly commodity ever created.

You work hard for it, but for your labors, you receive only pieces of paper carrying that one vague promise.

Though you worked for pieces of paper, and they cost the government virtually nothing to produce, the government wants them back. Why does a government that can print paper without cost, ask its citizens to return their hard-earned paper in the form of taxes? The answer will surprise you.

You will learn how we can free the vague promise from the obsolete thinking that limits its availability and its use. You will learn how we can *free money.*

If all this seems a nebulous and impractical flight of fancy, you are about to experience a revelation.

## *Chapter 1. -- What Do You Know and Why Do You Know It?*

*"Twenty-five years ago, atmospheric scientists fretted about global cooling. Today scientists agree that Earth's surface is warming . . ." Elizabeth Royte,* Discover Magazine, *February 2001*

*"Uncle Sam's revolving debt is crowding out the private sector . . . in addition to the government taking money away from other would-be borrowers, the increased demand results in rising interest rates choking off investment in buildings and machinery and reducing job creation . . . The United States is saddled with slow growth in productivity and high, long term interest rates . . . an unconstrained federal deficit (will) lead to high interest rates and eventually high inflation." Congressman Nick Smith, 1995,* Insight Magazine

*"A late surge of buying boosted blue-chip stocks to record highs . . . Economy glows. Inflation low."* Chicago Tribune, *September 1997.*

### The Golden Rule of Economics

It's been said, the Bible can be summarized in one sentence, "Do unto others as you would have others do unto you." All else is elaboration. Yet elaboration seems a part of the human psyche, as witness the many books, arguments and wars fought over religion.

The reason to free money can be summarized, "*A growing economy must have a growing supply of money.*" All else is elaboration. Yet, that thought has spawned perhaps the most complex, convoluted reasoning in all of science. This book is an attempt to return to reality.

We humans we have been on this earth for thousands of years. Yet within the past two centuries, the sum of human knowledge has grown exponentially, and in the past fifty years total available information has exploded.

Several factors combine to cause this growth. They relate to *the speed of information exchange*. The invention of the printing press and movable type allowed ideas to be disseminated faster and on a greater scale. Then came faster means of travel: the railroad, automobile and airplane, and faster means of communication: radio, telephone and television and Internet. Computers allow for fast development and exchange of theories and proofs.

Information exchange, the key to learning, means someone communicates a fact, idea or opinion to others, who are prepared to consider its worth. Were the transferred information rejected, there would be no "exchange" and no net gain in knowledge.

**Who Are the Leech Doctors?**

The fact that we know so much *more* is well understood. Sometimes less realized is the fact that we know so much *different.* Every generation believes it knows the Truth and resists seeing Truth disproved.

Aristotle, one of history's greatest thinkers, was wrong about how the world was constructed. There is more than earth, air, fire and water.

Before the great Copernicus, people believed the sun, moon and stars revolved around the earth. Not only could a scientist of the day lose his reputation if he disagreed, he could lose his life to the experts – religious leaders who felt threatened by ideas. Little has changed, for even today, many experts feel threatened by ideas.

More recently, doctors knew most diseases were caused by "bad" blood. The logical approach was to apply leeches to drain blood from patients, who were harmed, not cured, by the gruesome treatment. Even empirical evidence (the patients died) did not change the beliefs of the doctors, who continued to administer their "cure."

My high school basketball coach assured me the best therapy for sore muscles was the immediate application of hot packs. That was yesterday's Truth. Today's Truth: The best treatment is the immediate application of ice. Will that change tomorrow?

I also was told that drinking water during exercise will cause cramps. Today, I'm told that *not* drinking will cause cramps.

Of course, the past was inhabited by old-fashioned people. Such obvious errors could not be made in the informed, scientific, computerized, Internetted world of today. Or, could they?

Yesterday's Truth: Stomach ulcers were caused by emotional stress, which meant they never could be cured. Ulcer pain caused emotional stress, which in turn caused ulcers, an endless and medically lucrative circle.

Now, generations after the introduction of microscopes and antibiotics we have today's Truth: Most stomach ulcers are caused by the bacterium H pylori, and are cured by an antibiotic. All those ulcer medicines (Tagamet, et al), for which people spent billions to receive marginal relief, now provide marginal relief for heartburn.

How could our advanced medicine, with its microscopes that can resolve a single atom, not have discovered earlier that a big, old bacterium causes stomach ulcers? No one thought to look. The belief in stress as the cause was so widespread and accepted, it blinded those who otherwise might have questioned it.

Yesterday's Truth: Silicone breast implants cause a wide range of diseases. Class action suits abounded, and an army of experts, with impressive initials behind their names, testified about the horrors of silicone implants.

Today's Truth: Thanks to Dr. Marcia Angell, the executive editor of the *New England Journal of Medicine*, the medical world took a second look. A series of scientific studies tells us silicone implants carry few if any, long-term side effects. Once again, the experts were wrong (unless, of course, they are wrong *now*.)

The point: If the experts were wrong then, they could be wrong now. And if repetition can implant an erroneous theory, perhaps repetition can rip it out.

**Universal Truths – Which Do You Believe?**

Which of these Truths do you accept?

1. The U.S. federal debt is too high; It burdens taxpayers.
2. A growing federal debt is inflationary.
3. The savings rate in America is too low.
4. Americans have too much personal debt.
5. A growing federal debt forces interest rates up.
6. Low interest rates make borrowing easier, which helps the U.S. economy grow.
7. The U.S. trade deficit is too high and should be reversed into a trade surplus.
8. Taxes are necessary to pay for federal spending.
9. Business should pay its fair share of federal taxes.
10. There is no affordable solution to rising crime, health care and Social Security costs, poverty, military needs, a declining ecosystem and a deteriorating infrastructure.

**Stop and Think:** Which of these beliefs do you share? Note on a sheet of paper *why* you accept them. Which, do you not accept? Note why. Save this sheet of paper in your "Stop and Think" file.

You have followed the "Stop and Think" directions. You have identified some of your beliefs and even have preserved them on paper. You have thought about why you hold them.

*Now, can you accept the possibility that every one of the ten preceding statements is wrong?*

## A Letter From Congressman John Porter

On July 15, 1993, I received a letter from Congressman Porter (Illinois) in which he made these statements:

> "(Reducing the national debt) will stop the process of mortgaging our children's and grandchildren's future . . ."
> "I believe currency is (not a form of debt but) a medium of exchange."
> "I do not believe a reduction in public debt necessitates a reduction in money supply."
> "Increases in the money supply help spur increased economic activity, but they also help increase the rate of inflation."
> ". . .high (interest) rates restrict access to capital."
> "Sluggish growth is due in large part to the enormous debt -- individual, business and public -- hanging over the economy."
> "We must balance our budget and reduce our national debt."

Here you have a set of universal Truths as expressed by a respected politician back in 1993.

**Stop and Think:** Based on what you know happened to our economy since 1993, do you agree with Congressman Porter? Did the federal debt increase? Was there an increase in the money supply, and if so, did it parallel an increase in inflation? Did we have high interest rates? Did we have sluggish economic growth? Was there restricted access to capital?

I mentioned, "cognitive dissonance," believing two opposing ideas. Some misunderstandings about our economy arise from cognitive dissonance. I'll repeat two of the above statements, each of which has gained wide acceptance:

1. The U.S. federal debt is too high; It burdens taxpayers.
3. The savings rate in America is too low.

**Stop and Think:** Do you agree? Do you see any "cognitive dissonance" in those two statements? Consider what constitutes the federal debt and what constitutes savings.

The government accumulates federal debt when it sells Treasury bonds, notes and bills.

One of the most common, safest, most recommended forms of saving is the purchase of Treasury securities.

Every time you purchase a savings bond you support the increase in the federal debt. If we decrease the national debt, we will reduce the availability of the most reliable savings devices in America. Now do you see any contradiction?

Consider these common ideas:

1. The U.S. federal debt is too high.
4. Americans today have too much personal debt
6. Low interest rates make borrowing easier, which helps the U.S. economy grow.

Do you see any cognitive dissonance?

**Question:** How do low interest rates help our economy grow?

**Conventional wisdom**: Low interest rates make borrowing cheaper.

**Q**: Why does cheaper borrowing help our economy grow?

**CW**: In two ways. Cheaper borrowing allows business to borrow more, and pay less to obtain funds for expansion. And cheaper borrowing allows consumers to borrow and buy more. Strong consumer purchasing and business expansion make our economy grow.

**Q**: Does cheaper borrowing create more or less debt?

**CW**: The very purpose of cheaper borrowing is to encourage borrowing, and to create more debt.

**Q**: If low interest rates and easy borrowing are considered *good* for our economy, why are the "high" federal debt and "high" private debts considered *bad* for our economy?

Cognitive dissonance.

**The Eight Premises**

This book, which suggests alternatives to the current conventional wisdom, is based on eight premises:

1. The intuitive, quasi-religious appeal of conventional wisdom can hide logical defects and opposing evidence.
2. A theory that disagrees with empirical evidence, or one that is internally inconsistent (cognitive dissonance), must be replaced by a theory that agrees with empirical evidence and is internally consistent.
3. Familiar words used to describe a process in one field may mislead when used to describe a different process in a different field.
4. When the federal debt has grown rapidly, inflation has not grown.

5. When the federal debt has grown rapidly, the economy has grown.
6. When the federal debt grew rapidly, there has been no shortage of money for lending or spending.
7. Business is healthier in a growing economy than in a static or shrinking economy.
8. *A growing economy must have a growing supply of money.*

**Stop and Think:** Note on a sheet of paper, with which of the above premises you agree and with which you disagree. Why?

**Summary:** One purpose of this chapter was to continue what began in the Introduction -- the effort to open your mind to the *possibility* that some of what you believe may be wrong. The other purpose was to introduce you to new concepts that might challenge your current beliefs.

If this were a mystery book, I would say you now have all the clues necessary to solve the puzzle. You might want to review what I've told you thus far, to see if you can begin to develop your own theories about our economy. See if anything new comes to mind.

## *Chapter 2. -- What Is Money? I'll Bet You Have No Idea.*

*"There's a great debate among economists as to how you actually properly measure the money supply . . . There are things like credit cards. Some even question whether food stamps are part of the money supply . . ." Rita McDermott Mayer,* The World and I, *November 1996*

*"For every debit there is a credit." Accounting rule*

### What Are the Federal Debt and Deficit?

The U.S. federal *debt*, the net amount of *money* owed by the U.S. government, exceeds six trillion dollars. The federal debt grew because of the federal *deficit* – the annual excess of federal spending over federal tax income.

When we reduce our deficit, our federal debt continues to grow. To reduce our federal debt, tax income must exceed the spending outflow (a federal budget surplus).

**Stop and Think:** A federal surplus occurs when the government takes more money out of the economy than it puts in. List all the ways this benefits the economy. List all the ways this injures the economy.

The belief that the debt is too high is based on two concerns: "financial burden" and inflation. "Financial burden" describes the perceived difficulty our government could have in obtaining sufficient money to satisfy its financial obligations.

Personal experience teaches: When you borrow money, you must pay back the principal plus interest. These payments constitute a financial burden. If the financial burden is too great, you will be unable to meet it, and the result is bankruptcy.

Using personal experience leads to the conventional wisdom:

1. Government principal and interest payments place a financial burden on the economy. As federal debt grows, interest payments grow, and these interest payments add to the federal debt, requiring even higher interest payments.

   Principal and interest payments can overwhelm the government's ability to pay. When the government's debt obligations grow large enough, the government will be forced into bankruptcy.
2. Future generations will be born into debt. Even today, every American child is born owing more than $20 thousand, its share of the national debt. These future generations will be burdened by taxes to service the debt.

> **Stop and Think:** What is your opinion regarding points #1 and #2? Do you agree or disagree? Why?

**What Does the Government Do When It Runs Out of Money?**

When you or I owe more money than we earn, we might need to sell our assets – our home, our stocks, our car -- to pay our debts. We might even conduct a tag sale in our front yard.

The government does the same thing. When tax revenues fall short, the government sells its assets. No, the government does not sell Mount Rushmore or the Supreme Court building. The government sells Treasury bonds, notes and bills.

People who buy T-securities send money to the government, and they receive a credit to their account, which shows they own these debt instruments.

Like all debtors, the U.S. government owes money to its creditors, most of whom are U.S. taxpayers. Our "financially burdened" future generations are wealthy creditors, and the federal debt is money in yours and your children's pockets. That's why you buy government securities.

> *The economies of the world form a perfect balance sheet. For every debt, there is a credit; for every deficit, there is a surplus; for every lender there is a borrower; for every outflow, there is an income; for every sale there is a purchase.*

When the U.S. government runs a deficit, who runs the surplus? The answer: primarily the U.S. economy. ("Primarily" because other countries also receive money from the U.S. government.)

**How Big a Financial Burden Is the Federal Debt?**

Visualize one path money takes:

1) You lend the government $10 thousand by purchasing a Treasury bond, note or bill. Ten thousand dollars flow out of our economy to the government.
2) The government uses the money to purchase goods and services. The money flows back to our economy.
3) The government levies taxes. Money flows from our economy to the government.
4) The government pays you, the owner of its securities, the principal plus interest. Money flows to our economy, plus interest.

**Question**: The same money flows back and forth between the government and our economy. When is either party "financially burdened?"

**Answer**: You are burdened when you pay taxes. The government never is burdened by its debt.

**Question**: But the government pays me the lender, more money than it borrowed, in the form of interest. Is that interest a financial burden to the government?

**Answer:** No. The government always is able to borrow from you. The obligation is not a "burden," because the U.S. government never experiences difficulty obtaining all the money it needs to pay its debts. During years when the federal debt increased at a substantial rate, the government paid its debts without difficulty. *Without difficulty, there can be no burden.*

**Question:** Will future generations of taxpayers feel the burden?

**Answer:** *The only burden taxpayers feel is tax.* Taxpayers do not feel a burden from the federal debt, because they are not the debtors. They are the creditors. Creditors feel no burden.

During the past twenty years, government debt rose much faster than taxes. Had taxes declined, taxpayers would have felt even less a burden.

The notion that taxpayers must pay for government debt is false.

**Question:** Who pays for government debt?

**Answer:** The government pays its debt with borrowed funds.

**Question:** Is there a limit to what the government can borrow?

**Answer:** The federal debt rose from $910 billion in 1980 to more than $5+ *trillion* in 1996 -- almost a sixfold increase in sixteen years. Our economy was healthy, and there was no shortage of money to borrow.

The federal debt could rise another sixfold in sixteen years, and still there would be no shortage of money to lend the government. *There never can be a shortage of money to lend the government*, for reasons we will discuss.

**Question:** The amount of money lent to the government rose $4+ trillion. In addition, consumer debt rose. Is there a shortage of lending funds? Does government borrowing "crowd out" private investment?

**Answer:** Shortages of any commodity cause prices to rise. If there were a shortage of lending funds, the price of lending funds (interest rates) would rise as borrowers competed for the dwindling funds.

That did not happen. When the Federal Reserve Board anticipates inflation, it raises rates.

Despite the massive increase in borrowing, there is no shortage of lending funds, nor can there be.

If economics were astronomy, "crowding out" would be the flat-earth theory.

**Question:** So where has all this additional lending money come from?

**Answer:** Borrowing *creates* lending funds. The more borrowing, the more lending funds become available.

> **Stop and Think:** What is money? How is it created? How is it destroyed? Who determines how much money exists? Where did the extra $4 + trillion the government borrowed, come from?

**Which of These are Money?**

A dictionary definition of money is, "something generally accepted as a medium of exchange." What is "generally accepted?" What is a "medium of exchange?"

How is money different from "non-money"? Which of the following items do you consider money?

☐ Wheat a farmer exchanges for all his needs, from sausages to screwdrivers

☐ Fur pelts

☐ Oil

☐ Diamonds

☐ Gold

☐ Corporate stock

☐ Corporate bonds

☐ Your house mortgage

☐ Your personal bank checking account

☐Your money market account

☐ Your bank savings account

☐ Your credit card balance

☐ Travelers' checks

☐ U.S. Treasury securities

☐ A U.S. dollar bill

Did you have any difficulty with this list? Did you change your opinion at any point?

> **Stop and Think:** What criteria did you use when you differentiated "money" from "non-money?" List these criteria and file them in your "Stop and Think" file.

Money began as a replacement for barter. People traded goods or services for other goods or services. Barter requires a rare coincidence. Each party must want the other party's goods or services.

You sell boxes. I sell hats. We can deal only if I want boxes and you want hats. If I want bags rather than boxes, we can't trade.

For convenience, there evolved agreement that specific goods would generally be accepted as media of exchange. Gold and silver are the most familiar recent examples, although through the centuries, many objects were used as money. These included seeds, furs, stones, beads, woven goods, cigarettes – almost everything.

As the pace of transactions grew, physical products became unwieldy. Today, the world relies on no physical product, not even gold, to function as money.

Still, there is no agreement about the definition of money, even among experts. Most current definitions are too restrictive, and do not take into account the realities of world trade.

Examine some obvious forms of money. All U.S. coins and currency are money. "A U.S. dollar bill" should be checked on your list. U.S. dollars are a medium of exchange accepted almost everywhere.

The government has many definitions of money, which it codes, "M1, M2, M3, and L."

M1 includes currency, coins, demand deposits, travelers' checks from nonbank issuers, and other checking deposits.

M2 equals M1 plus overnight repurchase agreements issued by commercial banks, overnight Eurodollars, money market mutual funds, money market deposit accounts, savings accounts and time deposits less than $100,000. (Why $100,000? Just an arbitrary number. All definitions of money are arbitrary.)

M3 equals M2 plus institutionally held money market funds, term repurchase agreements, term Eurodollars, and large time deposits.

L is an obsolete term, but once equaled M3 plus Treasury bills, commercial paper, bankers, acceptances, and certain liquid assets such as savings bonds. Why not Treasury notes and bonds? They are less liquid (less easily converted to M1).

The government's current definitions of money require liquidity within one year. Treasury bonds maturing within a year are included; bonds maturing later are not included.

Why one year? This too is arbitrary.

Regardless of liquidity, *all the "M's" and "L" are debt and all are money.*

M1 includes *currency* and something that looks different from currency: *checking account balances*. If you write a check, your bank will give your creditor currency, limited by what you have in your account. Checks are a quasi-equivalent of currency. They are generally accepted media of exchange.

Sometimes checks even are more accepted than currency (for the payment of large debts) and sometimes less accepted (if there is concern the check might bounce.) You should have a check mark next to "personal bank checks."

| *A bank deposit is a bank debt.* |
|---|

**Question:** Who owns the money in your checking account?

**Answer:** I do.

**Q**: If you own it, how did your bank get it?

**A**: I gave it to the bank.

**Q**: No, you didn't *give* it to your bank. That would be a gift, and your bank would own it. You lent your

> money to your bank, with the stipulation that you can have it back whenever you write a check.
>
> You don't charge your bank interest for this loan (banks do pay interest on some checking accounts), but you require them to perform certain services in lieu of interest, such as processing your checks, sending you reports, etc.
>
> When you open a checking account, you are the creditor and your bank is the debtor.
>
> Your bank calls the money it owes you a "deposit."
>
> Your bank is able to boast about the size of its deposits. For psychological reasons, it does not boast about the size of its debts, though "deposit" and "debt" are identical.

The government's classification of money, "M2," includes everything in M1 plus *bank savings accounts, money market accounts, and certain bank related paper*. Why does a bank savings account receive a different classification from a bank checking account?

The money in a bank savings account is less liquid than the money in a checking account. Liquidity itself is not a criterion for money. It merely affects the classification.

Your savings account is a loan to your bank (also called a "deposit"), but in contrast to your checking account, you *do* charge the bank interest. Make sure you have a check mark next to "bank savings account."

The government has, at one time or another, included in their definitions of money: everything in M2 plus accounts in *savings and loans* associations, *money market* accounts and all the various types of *bonds* including U.S. savings bonds and *Treasury bonds, notes* and *bills* and bonds issued by corporations.

The differences among the words, "bonds," "notes" and "bills," when applied to government debt, indicate the term of maturity. Treasury bonds mature in ten to thirty years. Treasury notes mature in ten years or less. Treasury bills mature in one year or less. Otherwise, they all are loans to the government.

(When a 30-year Treasury bond reaches, in its 29th year, it equals, in liquidity, a newly issued Treasury bill, and becomes part of "L.")

Because all have quasi-equivalence with currency, they sometimes are referred to as "near money." This is misleading. They are not *near* money. They are money, the major difference among them being liquidity. Put check marks next to each.

Why has the government classified such different entities -- currency, checking and savings accounts, money market accounts, bonds issued by governments and bonds issued by corporations -- as money? And why are the other items in the list -- the wheat, pelts, oil, diamonds -- not considered money today?

And what about gold? Why is gold not considered money by the federal government? What elements are common to all the definitions of money?

**Stop and Think:** What criteria are common to the checked items but absent from the others? In what economic ways is a fur pelt different from a Treasury bond?

## The Four True Criteria for Money

Because of confusion about the definitions of money, questions about money itself also cause confusion:

Does our economy contain too much money? Too little money? Does too much money cause inflation? Does a growing federal debt make our government short of money?

How is money created? Who creates money? Is money ever destroyed? If so, how and why?

Until we agree on a definition and criteria for money, these questions make no sense. The definition and criteria must be consistent and appropriate to reality.

Here are the most logical, most useful criteria for money in today's economy. I suggest money must meet *all four* of the following criteria, and that everything meeting all four criteria is money.

1) *Money must be defined in a standard unit of currency.* A $10 bill, a $1 thousand treasury bill, a $50 bank account, all are defined by a fixed standard unit, the U.S. dollar.

A bushel of wheat is not defined by a standard unit of currency. A bushel of wheat has a *price*, but that price changes. One thousand dollars' worth of wheat today is not the same as one thousand dollars' worth of wheat tomorrow. There is no entity called, "$1,000 wheat."

However, a $1 thousand bank account today is identical to a $1 thousand bank account tomorrow, not in purchasing power, but in dollar denomination.

2) *Money has no intrinsic value*, no physical use. That is a second reason why wheat is not money. Nor are manufactured goods.

Though such goods may be exchangeable for currency, their value is intrinsic, not monetary. These products have a physical use that determines their demand and price. "Money" is not used for anything except . . . money.

Once, gold was used as money *and* it had intrinsic value. However, gold's intrinsic value bore no relationship to its money value. Price changes in gold had little to do with its functional use as a metal, and everything to do with gold's exchangeability for currency.

Today, gold cannot be exchanged for currency in the U.S. It is illegal to own it, unless you are a jeweler, a dentist, an electronics manufacturer or in some other business that needs gold for its *intrinsic* uses. Therefore, gold flunks the "intrinsic" test.

(The value of *recently minted* gold coins, like Krugerrands, is based on the intrinsic value of their gold content. The value of *rare* gold coins is not based on the value of gold, but rather on the supply and demand for that coin as a collectable. Though silver costs less than gold, some rare silver coins are worth more than gold coins.)

Until recently, many forms of money did have intrinsic value. But in 1971, when President Nixon took America off the metal standard, we freed ourselves from the ambiguity of evaluating money on both its intrinsic and monetary worth.

Because money has no intrinsic value, *a shortage of any raw material, or the lack of any production facility, never can cause a shortage of money.*

In its physical form, money is printed paper. Most money is even less physical than that. It's computer records, with a physical reality at the atomic level. The supply of money never is affected by such physical considerations as production, storage or transportation.

3) *The demand for money is determined by its risk (danger of default or devaluation, i.e., inflation) and its reward (interest rates).*

The value of any product, including money, is based on the supply and the demand for that product. Money has no necessary physical presence, so an unlimited potential supply always exists.

4) *Money must be owned by an entity other than the entity that created it.* When the federal government prints dollar bills, they are not money until they are issued. Even were the Treasury to hold trillions of sheets of printed dollar bills in a basement storage facility (perhaps it does), these dollar bills would have no money value until they were owned by some entity other than the Treasury.

No bond is money until it is purchased by someone other than the issuer (borrower). A corporation may have printed billions of dollars in unsold bonds. They are pieces of paper. They become money when they are sold and they cease being money when they are redeemed (purchased) by the corporation.

You might go to a dozen banks, obtain blank mortgage forms and fill them out. None of them becomes money while the form is in your hands. When a bank purchases one of your forms, your mortgage becomes money.

Your mortgage ceases to be money, when you buy it back, that is, when it once again is owned by you, the issuer.

Study the four factors describing money. Make sure you understand them, because they lead us to an important concept:

*These four criteria -- defined in a standard unit of currency; no intrinsic value; demand determined by risk and reward; not owned by its creator -- define money and also define financial debt.*

Like money, debt is defined in a standard unit of currency. Corporate, municipal and Treasury bonds, mortgages, even leases on cars and buildings are defined in U.S. dollars.

Your house mortgage may be your largest debt. You sold your mortgage to your bank. You signed and delivered your mortgage and your bank gave you a check. You are the mortgage creator.

Notice the parallel between what you did and what the U.S. government does when it sells Treasury bonds, notes and bills. In each case, a note went in one direction and another form of money went in the other direction.

For the next twenty years, you will buy your mortgage back from the bank. You will give the bank your currency or your check, and the bank will give you credits against your mortgage. Meanwhile, the bank might sell its remaining ownership of your mortgage to some other entity.

*All money is created by a borrower.* A borrower sells a note to a lender. At the time of sale, that note becomes money.

**Stop and Think:** When you signed your mortgage and delivered it to the bank, the bank gave you money. Did the total amount of money in the U.S. economy rise, fall or stay the same? Why?

The value of debt is determined by its supply and demand. The demand for debt is determined by risk and reward (interest). The higher interest a bond pays, the more demand for it. The greater the risk that principal and interest will not be paid timely or will depreciate in value (inflation), the less demand for the debt. The demand for a debt represents a compromise between its risk and its reward.

"Redemption value" is the amount the debtor will pay at the moment the debt matures. Before redemption, a bond may sell at above or below redemption value, depending on how potential buyers view the risk, the reward and the amount of accumulated interest.

A dollar is worth a dollar. But the value of a dollar (which carries no interest) varies with market conditions.

**When Are Financial Debt and Money the Same Thing?**

Money and financial debt have the same definitions. Thus, *all money is financial debt.* Debt and credit are two sides of the same coin. The owner of debt is called a "creditor."

***All money is debt.***

At this point you should hear a drum roll or a thunder clap. When you understand and accept this simple four-word statement, you will eliminate most misunderstandings about economics. Seeing that all money is the debt/credit twins, puts you ahead of the majority, including most of the U.S. Congress and even the economic writers in vogue.

Certain debts are not related to money. These are *non-financial* debts. When a *commodity* is owed, no money is created. If you borrow your neighbor's car, you have not created money. Even if you give your neighbor your written receipt -- an IOU saying "I promise to return your 1995 Ford . . ." – and your neighbor used that sign of debt as though it were a less-liquid form of money, you still have not created money.

The car is not money, nor is the receipt. Neither is denoted in a standard unit of currency. The car has intrinsic value, so the receipt, which represents the car, also has intrinsic value.

Commodity debts do not fit the definitions of money.

*"Credit," "debt" and "money" all refer to the same thing..*

Money consists of a receipt, a "debt instrument." There are many forms of receipts or debt instruments. A dollar bill is one.

Bonds and notes are debt receipts. They may be paper or electronic. Checking account and savings account electronic balances are nonphysical debt receipts and are money.

Consider the way this chapter began: "The U.S. federal *debt*, the net amount of *money* owed by the U.S. government . . ." When you first read it, you did not find anything wrong with that statement. Yet the statement equates debt with money. Did you realize that?

Though all your money is part of your wealth, all your wealth is not money. Your house, your car, your personal possessions are not money. This much we can say however:

*All other factors being equal, the more money you have, the greater your wealth.*

That seems obvious. Yet it is an important concept, the significance of which will become clear when we discuss the wealth and health of the world's economies.

**Stop and Think:** If all money is credit, how is currency – the fundamental money -- a form of credit? When you hold that dollar bill in your hand, are you a creditor? If so, who owes you the money? What kind of money do they owe you? How and when will you be paid?

U.S. dollars, have no intrinsic value and are backed only by the "full faith and credit" of the U.S. government. The words, "full faith and credit" indicate an obligation to pay, which is a definition for debt.

According to the U.S. Department of the Treasury (Brochure titled, "Fundamental Facts about U.S. Money," Dec. 1993):

> "The Federal Reserve Act requires that adequate backing is pledged for all Federal Reserve Notes in circulation. U.S. Treasury securities, acquired through open market operations, are the most important form of collateral and provide backing for most of the value of the currency in circulation."

The backing for currency is debt -- not land, buildings or any other assets -- just debt.

Look at the front of a dollar *bill* and you will see the words, "Federal Reserve *Note*." "Note," "bill" and "bond" all are names for debt instruments.

As the holder of a dollar bill you are a creditor to the U.S. government. You hold a debt instrument of unlimited term, paying 0% interest, and signed by the Secretary of the Treasury and the Treasurer of the United States.

In exchange for those dollar debt instruments, the U.S. government, will give you a Treasury bond, note or bill. These three debt instruments also can be exchanged for currency and also have no intrinsic value.

The Treasury bond, note and bill do pay interest and have limited terms, but otherwise are identical to dollars. They are backed by the same "full faith and credit," and nothing else.

> *Money is the ultimate "free lunch." To create a $100 bill, the government prints a piece of paper green, and magically this green piece of paper, backed only by the mystical "full faith and credit," is worth $1 - $500. Money is free.*

The fact that money is a free lunch bothers some people, because they had been inoculated with the idea there is no such thing as a free lunch. They also had been told, "If it sounds too good to be true, it probably is."

These clever little aphorisms masquerade as knowledge. They give the speaker the impression he/she has said something sage, while eliminating the effort of thought. In fact, there are free lunches; my mother fed me many. And my wife may sound too good to be true, but she's real.

And then there's free money. It's a free lunch and it sounds too good to be true, but it's true.

I mention this to remind you to think about the facts, and not be swayed by slogans, aphorisms and past prejudices.

**What does the U.S. government owe you, the holder of a dollar?**

Years ago, the government issued "Silver Certificates," which resembled today's dollars and functioned in the same way. These certificates were backed by silver rather than just full faith and credit. You could redeem them for silver.

One day the government said, "From now on, we owe you only 'full faith and credit.'" There is no other "thing" backing the U.S. dollar or any U.S. money.

Many people think U.S. federal credit is backed by such government assets as land, buildings and other physical properties. I once saw an article saying that when the federal debt exceeds the value of U.S. government property holdings, this country will go bankrupt.

Rank nonsense. There is no relationship between the government's property holdings and the value of a dollar or the solvency of the government. If the government gave away every building, acre or art object it owned, it would be neither one cent nearer to, nor further from, bankruptcy.

Why? First, no one knows the dollar value of the government's holdings. (What is Yellowstone Park worth? The Lincoln Memorial? The Pentagon? Lake Michigan?)

Second, no creditor is given the right to claim any of these properties. (Try telling the U.S. government you have a few million dollars and wish to redeem them for the Washington Monument.)

There is a group in America known as the Concord Coalition, whose stated purpose is to encourage a balanced federal budget. Concord maintains an E-mail discussion list in which I participated for several months.

The members resisted the notion that all money is credit. I repeatedly challenged them to think of a single type of money in America that was not credit. Each time, I received no answer.

On about the tenth occasion, I did receive an answer: "Monopoly money!" Clever.

**Stop and Think:** If government property holdings do not determine the value of a dollar, what does?

## *Chapter 3. -- How Is Money Created?*

The U.S. government has created all the U.S. government money in the world by printing it and selling it. "Printing and selling," in government terms, currently means "borrowing."

U.S. government money comes into circulation when the U.S. government sells it to a creditor. The money is a U.S. debt backed by the government's "full faith and credit." No other source of *U.S. government* money exists, though there are many sources of other types of money in the U.S. and in the world.

Since all U.S. government money is credit, the U.S. federal debt could become zero only if all U.S. government money disappeared. Some naive people think it would be prudent and beneficial for the U.S. government to have no debt or at least to reduce its debt. However:

*An economy without debt is an economy without money.*

**Stop and Think:** List a balanced budget's probable effects on the money supply and on the economy.

Imagine you are the only person in America, and you own all the money in America: $10 thousand in currency. Your $10 thousand is a debt of the U.S. government, which owes you its full faith and credit. You are the creditor; the government is the debtor.

At that moment, the U.S. government has no money. Only you have money.

Imagine now that the government prints $10 thousand in Treasury bills and you buy them. You *deposit* with the government your $10 thousand in currency, and the government gives you its Treasury bills.

Your purchase of Treasury bills is identical with your opening of a savings account in your bank. You *deposit* money with the institution (your bank or the government) and the institution gives you a receipt (deposit receipt or Treasury bills). In each case, the institution is the debtor and you are the creditor.

Conventional wisdom admires large bank deposits and abhors large federal debt. Yet, they are virtually the same.

The one difference: If the bank were to run short of money to cover its debts, it might be forced into bankruptcy. When the federal government runs short of money, it creates more.

*Federal debt is safer than bank deposits*. That is why the Federal Deposit Insurance Corporation (FDIC) insures bank accounts, but banks do not insure T-bills.

**Question:** Since a Treasury bill and a bank account have no intrinsic value, what sort of value do they have?

**Answer:** Money value.

Any commodity may have two values: intrinsic value or money value. There is no alternative.

When you bought those Treasury bills, a remarkable multiplication took place. You sent the government $10 thousand worth of currency and the government sent you $10 thousand worth of Treasury bills.

You still own $10 thousand. Your money now is in the form of the Treasury bills you bought. It is backed by the same full faith and credit as was your currency. But the U.S. government also has $10 thousand in the currency you paid.

When the government sends that $10 thousand back into our economy to pay for goods, services, principal and interest, the $10 thousand becomes money.

Before you bought those bills there was $10 thousand in your imaginary economy. Now there is $20 thousand. You have $10 thousand and the government sent another $10 thousand into the economy.

When the government printed and sold you a Treasury bond, it increased the federal debt, and it printed money. That is how the government creates money -- that, and by printing currency.

(The Federal Reserve conducts buying and selling operations that add or subtract money from our economy. The Fed buys Treasury securities from banks and delivers money in the form of credits to the banks. This act creates money because the banks can use these credits as backing for loans, which creates more money.)

For every dollar's worth of credit the Federal Reserve creates, the banks create another nine dollars of money, when they repeatedly lend 90%of what they receive.

(To subtract money, the Federal Reserve sells Treasury securities and withdraws credits from the banks. For every dollar the Federal Reserve withdraws, the banks are forced to destroy another nine, because the amount they can lend is reduced.)

**How You Create Money**

Deposit $10 thousand into your bank savings account. Have you lost any money? No, you still have your $10 thousand, as evidenced by bank's records. But the bank too, now has your $10 thousand, which it circulates in our economy for loans and other investments.

Where there were $10 thousand in our economy, now there are $20 thousand. When you made that bank account deposit, you created a debt, and you helped the bank create money.

**Question:** If "full faith and credit" back U.S. government money, what backs the money your bank created when you made a deposit?

**Answer:** Mostly, the full faith and credit of your bank. Banks do not maintain sufficient financial assets to cover all of their debt. The first $100 thousand of your money is guaranteed by the U.S. government, which means you receive first the full faith and credit of your bank, and if that fails, the full faith and credit of the U.S. government. After the first $100 thousand, you rely on your bank's credit.

Should your bank fail, you would have a claim against such physical assets as the bank building, equipment, etc. These assets are worth a small fraction of your bank's debt, and for practical purposes, can be considered worthless.

Some people think a bank savings account is like a safe deposit box that pays interest. It isn't. Putting money in a safe deposit box creates no money. You transfer your money to the box, but receive nothing in return. The bank does not owe you anything.

Buy a corporate bond for $10 thousand. You have the same amount of money you had before, as evidenced by the bond's certificates.

But the corporation now has your $10 thousand in cash. You made a deposit of money in the corporation and the corporation gave you its receipt -- its bond – in exchange.

A corporation may own sufficient physical assets to back the money created when it sold you its bond – or it may not. Healthy service organizations, may have far more debt than physical assets.

If borrowing did not create money, no one would borrow. You lend money, because you can *give it while keeping it and earning more money on it* -- the opposite of what happens with a gift.

Why do you take out a mortgage on your house? To obtain money. Of course, you could *sell* your house to obtain money, but then you wouldn't have your house. Borrowing allows you to obtain money without giving up your asset – a sort of "have your cake and eat it too" arrangement. Since the bank does not give up money (It can use your mortgage as money), your borrowing creates money.

Money is not created when the item lent has intrinsic value, as when you lend your car to a friend. But imagine leasing a $20 thousand car from a car dealer. Had you paid cash, you would be $20 thousand poorer.

If you lease the car, you give the dealer your signed lease contract, which he can use as money. Owning your lease contract makes the dealer wealthier, but you are no poorer in terms of money. When you lease a car you create money.

**Question:** If I use money -- for example, a bond – as collateral when I borrow, have I still created money?

**Answer:** After you borrow, you still own the bond and in addition you own the money you borrowed. The lender owns your note. The bond exists as money, as does your note and the money lent to you. Yes, you have created money.

**T-bills and the Concord Coalition**

The Concord Coalition, that group dedicated to cutting the government's debt, maintains an E-mail list. I joined to let the opposition pick holes in my philosophy. It's a great exercise for anyone who has a belief they would like to test. Here is one of the posts I made on this list (Others are at the end of this book):

> "Many members of this list understand that government debt is money. Recently however, a member objected to defining T-bills as money. He said, 'I can't spend T-bills.'"
>
> "What this member really said was, Currency is the only form of money that can be spent. All other forms of money are less liquid than currency, with "liquidity" defined as convertible to currency.
>
> "Consider a savings account. You send $1,000 to your bank and the bank gives you a passbook entry stating you have $1,000. Do you now have less money? No, savings accounts are considered a form of money. They also are a form of debt, because the bank owes you the money.
>
> "Can you 'spend' your $1,000 savings account money? No. First, you must liquidate some of the debt by going to the bank and withdrawing currency. A withdrawal of money from your account is identical with cashing in a T-bill.
>
> "Some people might object that you don't need to withdraw currency. A checking account is like a savings account, except you can withdraw money by writing a check.
>
> "You cannot 'spend' a checking account. You must write a check, which liquidates part of the bank's debt to you, and orders the bank to transfer currency from its holdings to your designated recipient.
>
> "Writing a check is identical to cashing in a T-bill. Think of T-bills as 'government accounts,' similar to bank accounts. T-bills cannot be 'spent.' Nor can any other form of

money except currency, since all other forms of money represent currency.

"To deny that T-bills are money because they can't be 'spent,' is to deny there is any form of money except currency. Since T-bills are money, and meet all four criteria for money, the government's destruction of T-bills (by running a surplus) removes money from our economy.

"Do you see that running a government surplus destroys money? This hurts the economy."

The Concord Coalition members never answered.

## Is Corporate Stock Money?

**Stop and Think:** Stocks and bonds are investments. They both are traded. They vary in market value. We already know that bonds are money. So, are stocks money?

Stock represents the *intrinsic* value of the corporation. The demand for stock is determined by the perceived intrinsic value of the corporation.

Stock is not defined in a standard unit of currency. While a $10,000 bond always is a $10,000 bond, no matter what its current market price may be, shares of stock don't have a fixed redemption price. (The "par value" put on many stocks is a meaningless figure in today's economy.)

When you buy a bond from a corporation, you create a debt. The corporation owes you money. When you buy stock from a corporation, the corporation owes you nothing.

Corporate bonds are issued in standard units of currency, and the value is determined by the perceived *credit* of the company and the interest paid by the bond.

When the stock market goes up or down, the amount of debt in our economy does not change. Stock is not money, and the government does not classify it as such.

The Dow-Jones and Standard & Poor stock averages do not measure the amount of money in our economy, and so are not good indicators of the health of our economy. Prior to 1929, as the country headed toward the Great Depression, stock averages rose. But the amount of money in our economy did not rise with them, proof the economy was sick.

***The federal government ran a surplus (the economy ran a deficit) in the years prior to the Depression. The federal government destroyed money, which was the primary cause for the Depression.***

If Money Is Credit, Is Accounts Receivable Money?

Look for measures of money in the economy, and you seldom will see accounts receivable mentioned. Yet, A/R meets all the definitions of money. It is defined in a standard unit of currency (dollars.) It has no intrinsic value. Its demand is determined by risk and reward. Companies known as "factors" pay for A/R based on risk and reward. A/R is owned by an entity (the seller) other than the entity that created it (the buyers).

When a business makes a purchase, it creates an accounts receivable for the seller. The purchaser owns no less money, but the seller now owns a receivable, which he can convert into currency by selling it to a factor. The seller can use that accounts receivable as he would use any debt.

A buyer creates an accounts receivable to aid his *cash flow*. The accounts payable (from the buyer's perspective) substitutes for cash. An accounts receivable is money.

**Stop and Think:** When you buy $1 thousand worth of stock, you give your thousand dollars to the owner of the stock and he gives you the stock. If stock is not money, does that mean you lose your money the instant you exchange it for stock?

**What Is the Difference Between Money and Wealth?**

This question hints at a reason for confusion about money: the tyranny of semantics. In common vernacular, the phrase, "lose money," means a loss of *wealth.* Under that definition, you do not lose money the instant you buy a stock, because the stock is part of your wealth, as is your land, your crops, your gems, your antiques, your art work, your car, your house and, of course, your money.

If you were to fill out a personal balance sheet, all of these items would be considered part of your wealth, though not part of your money.

However, the word "money," as used in an economic sense, means something more specific. Wealth exists as money plus non-money assets.

The federal debt and deficit refer only to money. Therefore, every time you buy stock, you *do* "lose" money, though that loss is offset by a gain in another asset that contributes to your wealth. You "lose money" without necessarily losing wealth, when you purchase an item of intrinsic value.

## When Bond Prices Go Up, Does the Amount of Money Go Up?

> **Stop and Think**: If bonds are money, does the amount of money in our economy change when the bond market goes up or down? Why?

Money is credit. When the bond market goes up and down, the total amount of credit (the *redemption value* of the bonds) does not change. The amount of money in our economy does not change when the bond market goes up or down.

Assume you buy a bond with a face value (redemption value) of one $1 thousand. If the market value of your bond rises your wealth, would grow. However, since the amount of debt did not change, the amount of money did not change.

The *market value* of money does not affect the *amount* of money. Inflation, which reduces the market value of money, does not affect the amount of money.

> **Stop and Think:** You buy a "zero coupon" bond at a discount and at the end of its term, you redeem it for its face value. If you buy a zero coupon bond for a $1 thousand and in ten years it will be worth $2 thousand, how much money do you have when you buy the bond and when the bond matures?

When you buy the bond for $1 thousand, you receive a certificate worth $1 thousand in debt. That is how much money you have. In ten years, when you will be entitled to exchange that bond for $2 thousand, you will have $2 thousand, because the issuer will owe you $2 thousand.

The redemption value of most kinds of money rises through time, because of interest. U.S. savings bonds often have been of the zero coupon variety. You buy them at a low price and years later you redeem them at a high price.

At any given moment, you own in money, the amount the bond issuer (not an outside buyer) is required to give you if you redeemed it today -- that is, the amount of money at that time.

Because of myriad rules affecting the redemption of bonds, notes and bank certificates of deposit, the amount of money you own can vary. But this variance does not change the facts surrounding the creation and destruction of money.

The total amount of money in the economy equals the current redemption value (not market value) of all debt instruments.

**Stop and Think:** Bonds are money. Raising interest rates makes money more valuable, because higher interest rates increase the demand for money. Yet, when interest rates go up, the price of bonds goes down. How can this be?

Raising interest rates makes the market value of existing debt fall, *compared to the value of currency.* An investment with an interest rate fixed at 6% loses market value when the interest paid by other investments rises. The more years' worth of interest a debt has left to pay, the more the price will fall when interest rates rise.

Consider a Treasury note paying 6% and maturing in five years. When it matures, that note will be worth about 34% more than it is today. If the note matures at $1,000, you will pay about $747 for it. The $747 is its accumulated value. The other $253 is future interest.

## Economic Theories That Have Been Proven Wrong, Yet Remain Widely Believed

> **Stop and Think:** Does cutting tax rates help the economy? Under what circumstances might it help and when might it not help?

**Keynes:** Through thc years, economists have tried to equate money with economic growth. The theories of John Maynard Keynes held sway from the late 1930's through the 1960's. Keynesians called for "cheap" money (low interest rates) to stimulate investment and employment.

The demand for money is determined by risk and reward (interest). As the reward declines, the demand declines, which decreases the value of money.

This decrease is known as "inflation," and was the weakness in Keynes' strategy. Reducing interest rates can cause inflation, while doing little for economic growth.

**Friedman:** In the 1970's and 1980's, the "Monetarists," led by Milton Friedman, proposed that the steady growth of the money supply would provide for economic growth and low inflation. Friedman had an excellent idea, ruined by the wrong definitions for money, and no solution for inflation.

Had he included all forms of money in his equations, and specified interest rate control to prevent inflation, he would have come much closer to predicting what happened in our economy.

Today, the Fed seems to follow Keynes' strategy, but as a last resort leans toward Friedman. The Fed's uncertainty of strategy increases the uncertainty of our economy.

As this is written, the Fed has reduced interest rates by one half percent, attempting to prevent a recession. This follows two years of rate increases, attempting to prevent inflation.

However, inflation is not the opposite of recession. Using one tool to prevent them both, will not work.

**Laffer:** "Supply-side" economics favored tax cuts and also cuts in certain benefits, particularly to the unemployed. Cutting tax rates first helps the wealthy, who pay the highest rates. Cuts in unemployment benefits hurt the poor. These two factors gave the program its nickname: "Trickle-down theory."

The weakness of supply-side economics is its concern about a growing federal debt. The "Laffer curve" supposedly demonstrated that cutting tax rates would so boost the economy, total taxes collected would increase.

Supply-siders didn't recognize that cutting tax rates was not the fuel of economic growth. Rather, it was the growing debt -- increasing the money supply -- that boosted the economy. When the debt grew dramatically, the "Laffer curve" failed, though the economy prospered.

Cutting tax rates, while hoping the federal debt declines, is like taking aspirin for your heart, while hoping the aspirin doesn't thin your blood. The whole point of cutting tax rates is to put more money into the economy. If you collect more taxes, you've destroyed the concept.

**What Was President Nixon's Most Momentous Decision?**

During the Nixon administration, we at last cut ourselves loose from the gold standard. Some people remember President Nixon for opening trade dialogs with China. Others remember him for Watergate.

However, his most important act -- the act that changed the course of economic history -- came when he snipped the final threads binding the dollar to gold. Money supply no longer was limited by the supply of a scarce commodity. Money supply no longer had to be limited at all.

The fact that this happened only three decades ago, may be why "modern" economics has not yet caught up. Those economists who attended college prior to Nixon's greatest act, still operate under the old rules. They still think of money in obsolete terms.

Sadly, students of these economists are taught the same old "debt-is-bad" dogma.

## *Chapter 4. -- Why Do You Pay Taxes? Wrong!*

*"They (tax cuts) should not be presented as a way to prevent an economic slowdown . . . Reducing the national debt should remain a priority, because it cuts debt service and leaves the nation in better shape to deal with future unexpected economic challenges. . . The last thing President Bush should do is jerk the nation back into the dreary era of federal budgets scripted in red."* Editorial, Chicago Tribune, *January 22, 2001.*

You are about to learn something that not one person in a thousand understands. You will find it as counterintuitive as you found the revelation that credit is identical with money. You are about to learn the most important effect of taxation.

**Stop and Think:** Why does the federal government levy taxes? What would happen if the government did not levy taxes?

If you ask most people why the government levies taxes, they will tell you, "To pay for goods, services, entitlements and to pay its debt." If you ask most people what would happen if the federal government did not levy taxes, they would answer, "The government would go bankrupt." Are those your answers?

### Why Your Taxes Never Pay for Government Spending

The belief that federal taxes pay for goods, services, entitlements and government solvency, is behind the powerful "eliminate-the-debt" attitude, both in Congress and in the populace. This belief, though widespread, is false. Any belief that is both widespread and false, represents a grave danger.

Federal taxation does not pay for goods, services or entitlements. Federal taxation does not keep the federal government solvent (although as you will see, taxes do keep *state and local* governments solvent.)

Federal taxation has no benefits for our economy, for our government or for us -- no beneficial purpose at all. This pervasive, intrusive, much-hated, easily-abolished activity is worthless. Worse than worthless, it is harmful.

In year 2001, the government will spend $8.72 billion on the IRS. This does not include the many billions that business and individuals spend on preparing and filing tax records. The wasted government spending benefits the economy, but the wasted business hours are a loss.

**Stop and Think:** The federal government creates money when it sells Treasury bonds, notes and bills, and prints currency. Corporations create money when they sell bonds to creditors. You create money when you take out a mortgage and when you deposit money into bank and money market accounts.

How is money destroyed? Who does it?

## The Effect of Taxation Is to Destroy Money

When the federal government borrows, money is created and added to our economy. What happens when you pay taxes?

Assume your tax bill is $1 thousand. You send $1 thousand to the government. You become $1 thousand poorer, since you receive nothing in return.

The government uses your money to pay the interest and principal on $1 thousand worth of Treasury certificates. Because those certificates were issued by the federal government, they cease to be money the instant they again are possessed by the issuer. When you pay $1 thousand in taxes, the amount of money in our economy is reduced by $1 thousand.

Taxation has two monetary effects: to destroy money or to prevent the creation of money.

(It also has a social purpose. Taxes on liquor and cigarettes are attempts to limit their use. The social purpose is irrelevant to this discussion, though the taxes themselves do hurt our economy.)

When taxes pay for goods and services, the taxes substitute for the creation of the money that otherwise would have been needed to pay for those same goods and services.

*The sole effect of federal taxes is to destroy money, and/or to prevent the creation of money.*

Remember premises number seven and eight that we expressed in Chapter 1:

Premise 7: Business is healthier in a growing economy than in a static or shrinking economy.

Premise 8: *A growing economy must have a growing supply of money.* This is the Golden Rule of economics.

If I asked you, "How is your business doing?" your answer would be more positive if your business were growing. If I asked you, "How is American business doing?" your answer will be more positive if American business were growing.

There are numerous measures of American business and economic growth. (The words, "business" and "economy" are synonyms in a free-market. The state of our economy equals the state of our business.)

Gross National Product and Gross Domestic Product, are popular measures of our economy. Choose any measure you wish, and the result will be the same: American business is healthier in a growing economy. Were the GNP or the GDP to begin a downward trend, the country would be in a recession or a depression.

In general, does a large business need more money than a small business? The answer is obvious. General Motors must have more money to operate than does the corner tavern.

Does a large economy require more money than a small economy? Again the answer is clear. The economy of the United States of America must have much more money to operate than does the economy of California, which in turn, must have more money than the economy of Peoria.

Therefore we have inspected the last two premises and found them sound. Business is healthier in a growing economy, which requires the real supply of money to grow.

Some may argue that while a growing economy *requires* the real supply of money to grow, this doesn't prove that a growing real supply of money *causes* the economy to grow.

Adding money to an economy won't always cause immediate growth. Depending on circumstances, a money infusion only may inhibit a decline or collapse. For that situation, a greater infusion of money is needed.

As this is written, Japan is in that situation. Money is being added to its economy, enough to prevent a depression, but not enough to stimulate health. Japan needs significantly to increase money creation.

**What Kinds of Taxes Hurt Our Economy?**

Some may argue that adding money to an economy causes inflation. As we will discuss later, that is untrue. For now, we can agree that a growing economy must have the real supply of money grow, and the real supply of money can grow only if debt grows.

> *Because all taxes destroy money, all taxes hurt business and our economy.*

Taxes do not, cannot and will not ever help our economy. All federal taxes always hurt our economy by destroying money. Always.

Every federal tax levied on business takes money from business and from our economy, which diminishes the ability of business to pay salaries, to conduct research, to produce goods and services and to market them.

Every tax levied on individuals takes money from these individuals and reduces their ability to purchase, which then takes money from business and from our economy.

Politicians try to impose taxes that will encounter a minimum of public outcry. Yet all taxes, whether so-called "harmless" taxes on cigarettes or "heartless" taxes on medicine and baby food, have three identical economic effects:

1) All taxes destroy money.
2) All taxes hurt business.
3) All taxes hurt our economy.

Even the import duties business often begs for, take money from the private sector and pass it to the government, which weakens business.

**News Flash: For Every Debit There Is a Credit**

For every debit there is a credit. For every debtor there is a creditor. For every deficit there is a surplus.

When the federal government runs a deficit (creates money), our economy runs a surplus (receives money). When the government runs a surplus, our economy runs a deficit.

*A government deficit = an economic surplus;*
*A government surplus = an economic deficit.*

In the name of "fairness," business taxes have risen faster than personal taxes (as though business somehow competed with individuals for dollars, rather than being a supplier of dollars.) Sadly, labor union leaders have convinced their membership that "if it is good for business it must be bad for the workers."

These union leaders push for higher import duties and higher taxes on business, both of which harm American workers. Workers think import duties protect jobs. Import duties destroy jobs by removing money from the economy.

**Who Is Hurt by Taxes on the Rich?**

Another attempt at tax "fairness" involves over-taxing the rich. Yet the rich share our economy with the poor, and supply the jobs that feed the poor.

The more tax dollars taken from the rich, the more the poor are injured, because the government destroys those tax dollars. Trying to tax only the rich is like trying to drain only the northern half of a bath tub.

In a suffering economy, the poor suffer more. How ironic, that the poor cheer when taxes on the rich are raised. The poor do not realize they will be the losers.

Paying federal taxes does not help the federal government. Money is not scarce to the government, which year after year, continues to prove it can print (borrow) all the money it needs, without limit.

During the Reagan years, the amount of federal money rose rapidly, and our economy grew. Many people called this "false prosperity," because it relied on growing debt.

Growing federal debt is not false prosperity. It is prosperity.

**Stop and Think:** Since both history and reason show that all taxes hurt our economy, why does the federal government continue to tax? Think of why taxes came into existence. What form did the earliest taxes take? What is different about taxes today?

**Why Do You Pay Federal Taxes?**

Taxes began centuries ago, when "money" consisted of scarce barter goods, which had intrinsic value. The demand value of these goods depended on their scarcity (like precious metals and gems) and/or on their utility (like food, cloth and building materials.)

Ancient governments were not able to create acceptable money by printing it. They obtained money by taking physical goods from the populace -- the earliest taxation. Taxation became institutionalized.

Even with today's modern concept of money as credit, there remains the strong emotional bias against debt ("Neither a borrower nor a lender be.") Some religions even outlaw debt and interest, and in all societies debt has been associated with neediness and imprudence.

(Ironically, those religions and nations that outlaw debt include some of the wealthiest countries in the world. These people do not realize that all of their money is credit, and they have more of it than most. They load money into banks, which then *owe* the money to the depositor. As depositors, these people are lenders.)

What gives debt its bad name? The need to pay it back puts a financial burden on the debtor, and attempts to collect give the creditor a bad name (as in Shakespeare's *The Merchant of Venice).*

Debt symbolizes living beyond your means, buying things you cannot afford. So when government spending increases, "prudent" governments increase taxes, as a false guarantee of their ability to repay their loans.

This "prudence" makes sense for debtors who do not have the unlimited ability to create money. You an I are in that category. Money is a scarce commodity for us. But money is not scarce to the U.S. government, which can borrow all the money it needs.

**Stop and Think:** We have stated "Money is not scarce to the U.S. government, which can borrow all the money it needs." We did not substantiate this statement. Do you believe it? Why or why not?

Typical of the anti-debt bias is that statement by Representative Louise Slaughter, "We can't afford the debt we have. It means there is no capital for anybody to borrow, and just the interest on the debt is eating us alive."

She said it in 1993, when the federal debt was four trillion dollars. Three years later, the federal debt exceeded $5.3 trillion, a 30% increase. Yet, there was no shortage of capital to borrow in 1993, and there is no shortage today.

**Stop and Think:** If ever there were a shortage of capital to borrow, what would happen?

When there is a shortage of any commodity -- including capital – the price goes up.

A limited supply and sustained demand for money would cause lenders to raise prices (interest rates). Instead, interest rates declined after 1993.

Were you to ask Rep. Slaughter her opinion today, it may not have changed, despite the conclusive evidence she was wrong. Such is the power of conventional wisdom and cognitive dissonance.

**Stop and Think:** Why do people believe a "high" federal debt leads to a shortage of lending capital? What did Representative Slaughter mean by, ". . . just the interest on the debt is eating us alive?"

The November 1996 issue of *The World and I* magazine discussed a survey of the 700 members of the American Economics Association:

"A majority . . . believe that federal spending increases are the main culprit that fans the federal budget deficit blaze." Note the use of such prejudicial words as "*. . . culprit that fans the . . . blaze.*"

Four sentences later, the article gives the results of one question in the survey:

> "Q: 'Did the Reagan tax cut have the overall impact of increasing or decreasing economic growth?'
>
> A: Increasing growth, 81% (of the respondents said.) Decreasing growth, 19%.'"

What is happening? Why the talk about a "culprit" and "fanning the blaze" when discussing increased economic growth?

Consider this, from the same article:

> "Q: 'Do you think the next Congress ought to put a high priority on cutting taxes, on restraining expenditures, on both, or on neither?'
>
> A: Cutting taxes (alone), 0%"

Why did the experts who acknowledged President Reagan's tax cuts and ballooning deficits increased economic growth, also reject another tax cut? "

**Stop and Think**: What would happen to the U.S. economy if the federal debt rose more than 500% in the next sixteen years? Hint: Visualize the government selling massive amounts of money -- Treasury bonds, notes and bills. What will be the effect on our economy? On interest rates? On the government's ability to service its debt? On taxes? On inflation?

## *Chapter 5. -- When Will the U.S. Government Go Bankrupt?*

*"There is . . . no historical data that would demonstrate that a balanced budget enhances gross domestic product or any other indicator of economic productivity . . . On six consecutive occasions from 1817 until 1930, when government cut spending considerably without simultaneously seeking to stimulate the economy with equally deep tax cuts . . . depressions arose." Michael Johns,* The World and I, *April 1996*

*"If we choose wisely, we can pay down the debt, deal with the retirement of the Baby Boomers, invest more in our future and provide tax relief." President Clinton, January 18, 2001.*

Had anyone in 1980 announced that in sixteen years the U.S. federal debt would increase more than 500%, most experts would have predicted rampant inflation, depression, default on debt and the destruction of the world's financial system.

Experts in 1980 would have used the same arguments they now use when they bemoan the current federal debt. They would have been the first to demand a federal surplus.

As you have learned:

1) The federal debt rose more than 500% in sixteen years.
2) We did not have rampant inflation. Our inflation has been as modest as the Federal Reserve has wanted it to be.
3) We did not experience a depression, a default or the destruction of the world financial system. Our economy grew.

4) To legislate a balanced federal budget is to legislate against the creation of money.
5) Our economy today, being larger and stronger than it was sixteen years ago, has and must have more money than it did then.

**Stop and Think:** What would our economy be today if we had passed a Balanced Budget Amendment sixteen years ago? Why do you think so?

**What Will the Federal Surplus Accomplish?**

With a surplus, the U.S. government spends less than it receives. On net, the government destroys money.

Even with a balanced budget, the total *real value* of existing money declines due to inflation. If our economy contained $5 trillion dollars tomorrow and forever, even the most minuscule inflation would cause those $5 trillion to have a real worth of less than $5 trillion.

If inflation were but 2%, those $5 trillion would be worth, in constant dollars, $4.9 trillion in one year. After sixteen years, our economy would contain only $3.6 trillion in constant dollars.

We are geared to inflation. Experts feel a small amount of inflation creates the beneficial illusion that salaries and real-estate values are increasing.

If the real value of all the money in our economy declined, the entire economy would decline, and in a short time, we would enter a depression. It happened in the Great Depression. Workers lost their jobs. Businesses lost their profits. The value of real estate plunged -- all this from a federal surplus.

Taxes result from salaries, business profits and real estate holdings. A recession or depression causes tax collection to decline.

If the federal government were not allowed to create money, it could not pay its bills as tax revenues declined.

The government would be forced to increase tax rates, which further would destroy our economy. The federal government would go bankrupt, thanks to its balanced budget.

A federal surplus will be even worse.

**What Would Happen If the U.S. Debt Were to Grow 500% in Sixteen Years?**

Compare the above economy to an economy that increases its money 500% in sixteen years, with the same 2% inflation? That economy would have a real $18 trillion. In constant dollars, is a $3.6 trillion economy as strong as an $18 trillion economy? Obviously not.

What will happen to the U.S. economy if the federal debt rises 500% in the next sixteen years? We will continue to have whatever modest level of inflation the Federal Reserve wants, no depression, no default and no destruction of the world financial system. Our economy will grow larger and stronger than it is today. And yes, we will have more lending capital than ever.

Will the U.S. government service the $25 trillion debt it would have in sixteen years? Yes. The U.S. always repays its debts, right on schedule (unless Congress gets into a political hissy-fit of ignorance, as it sometimes has in the past, and refuses to approve a higher federal debt ceiling).

The U.S. repays its debts with U.S. dollars, the same money you use to repay your debts. Because U.S. dollars are credit, the U.S. repays its debt with credit/money, *the only money in existence.*

To service a growing debt requires an accelerated creation of money. Borrowing begets borrowing at a growing rate because of the need to cover interest. When the government borrows one dollar, it must pay back more than one dollar.

At current interest rates, and no change in spending or taxes, the U.S. federal debt would double in less than sixteen years. The government easily will service that debt.

*With inflation at 3% and interest at 5%, the government needs 8% more money each year, just to accomplish what it did the previous year.*

*Just to stand still we need a $16 trillion dollar debt in 2010.* Anything less requires that we have a recession or a comparable increase in non federal debt.

As our population grows and ages, many more people will require Social Security and Medicare payments. We have had a long period of relative peace and the end of the cold war. Though these conditions have allowed for a reduction in military spending, the situation will change.

It is unlikely the government will be able to limit its expenditures and to accomplish no more in future years than it does now.

**Can the Economy Grow If the Federal Debt Shrinks?**

**Stop and Think:** A shrinking federal debt reduces the amount of money the federal government creates. Can the economy grow if the federal debt shrinks?

For about twenty years after World War II, the federal debt remained flat, decreasing in certain years, while increasing in others. Yet the economy grew.

Question: How was this possible?

Answer: Federal debt is one part of *total debt.* At the end of World War II (1945) federal debt amounted to about 62% of total debt. We also had consumer debt, business debt and non federal (state, county, city, park district, school board, etc.) debt.

During the post World War II period, non federal debt rose substantially. Twenty years after World War II, federal debt amounted to only 26% of total debt. The rise in total debt supported the growing economy.

Graphs showing average annual changes in total debt and Gross Domestic Product reveal that the two tend to move together.

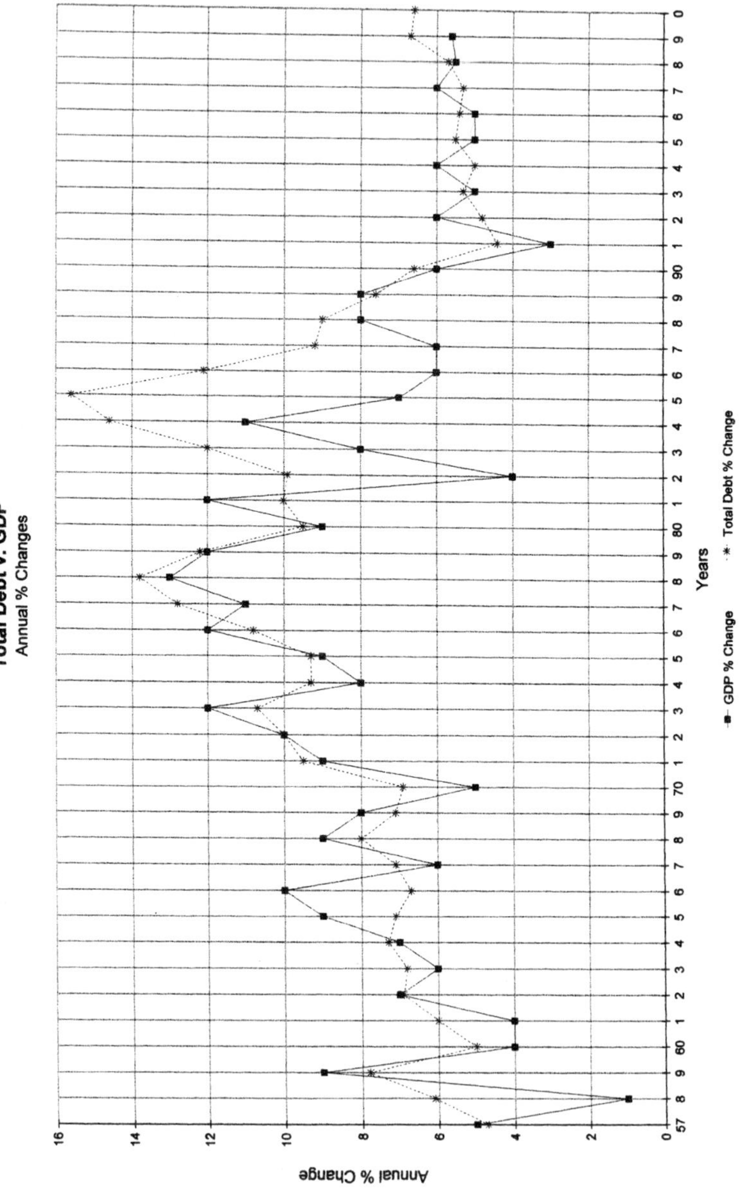
Total Debt v. GDP
Annual % Changes
Annual % Change
Years
GDP % Change
Total Debt % Change

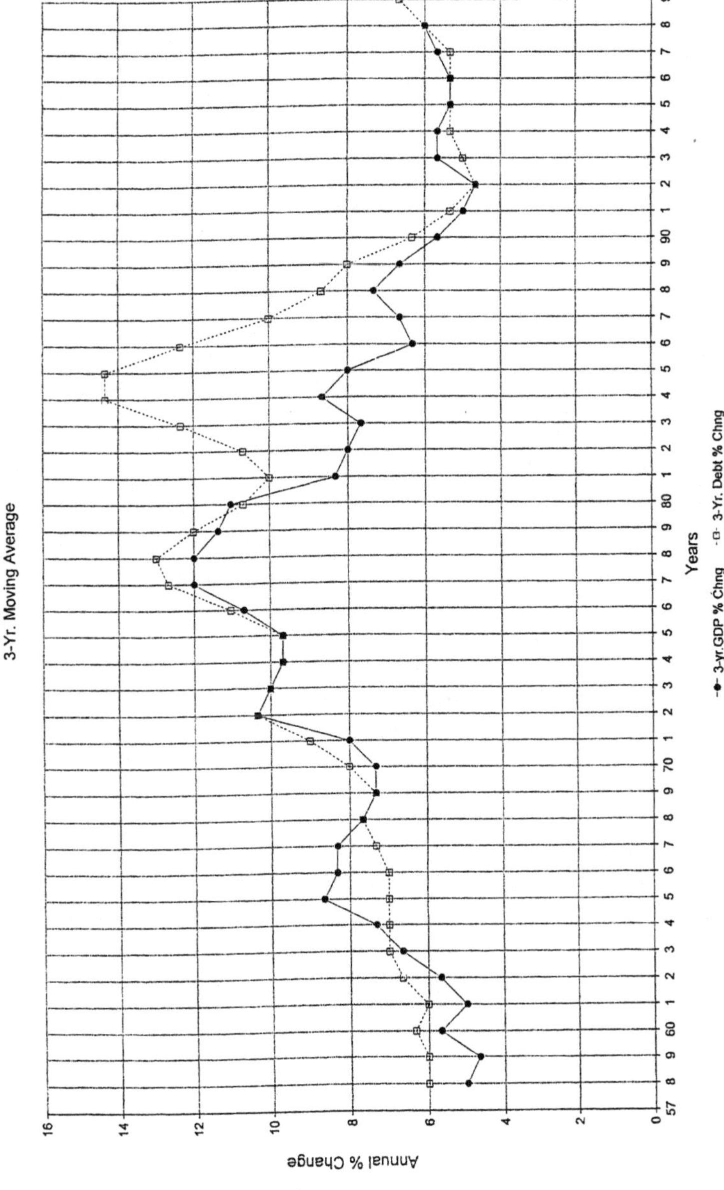
GDP v. Total Debt- Ann % Chg
3-Yr. Moving Average
Annual % Change
Years
3-yr.GDP % Chng
3-Yr. Debt % Chng

Consumer debt is an important part of total debt. The November 1, 1996 Economic Monitor (Huntington National Bank) said, "When consumer borrowing growth tapers off, so does overall economic activity. Each of the nine postwar recessions was preceded by a distinct slowing in credit."

There is no difference between federal debt and non federal debt. Money is money. So the key relationship to watch is total debt vs. GDP.

Even here, the correlation, though quite close, is not perfect. Our economy is so complex that cause and effect can be obscured by anomalies. In this, the economies of the world resemble the weather.

We know that temperature relates to day length. Yet, if you plotted any one year's, or even hundred year's, daily temperature in Chicago against day length, you would produce a graph resembling the total debt vs. GDP chart. There would be period-to-period inconsistencies (April 1 has not, on average, been warmer than March 28), but the overall relationship would be clear.

Economic growth requires *some* form of debt to increase. The federal government, having little control over the amount of non-federal debt, begins to lose control over the economy when federal debt declines.

Federal debt is safer than non federal debt, because only the federal government can create money at will to service its debts. In recent years, consumer borrowing grew faster than federal borrowing. Had consumers not been on their money-creation binge, the GDP would have risen less.

Federal control over the national economy requires the government to create money.

## How Can the Government Pay Its Debts?

The ability of you, the U.S. government and me to borrow depends partly on "credit rating." The higher your credit rating, the more you can borrow at the lowest interest rate.

An unlimited credit rating would permit you unlimited borrowing at the lowest interest rate. If you failed to repay in timely fashion, your credit rating would drop and you would have to pay a higher rate.

Unlimited borrowing always is possible so long as you pay a high enough rate. A person with bad credit can find a lender if he is willing to pay 100%, 500%, 1,000% or more per year. That is the basis for so called "juice loans." Mobsters lend to people of bad credit not only because the collection methods are effective, but because interest rates are high.

Your credit rating is based on lenders' beliefs about your *ability* and *willingness* to pay timely interest and principal. Neither city, nor county, nor state governments, nor you, nor I have an unlimited credit rating.

By contrast, the U.S. government has an unlimited credit rating. Lenders consider an obligation backed by the "full faith and credit" of the United States government to be essentially risk free.

Why? The U.S. never has defaulted on a debt, and the U.S. has an unlimited ability to create credit/dollars to pay its debts. The government has demonstrated both the ability and the willingness to pay timely interest and principal on any debt.

Further, the U.S. inflation rate has been modest, and the Federal Reserve Board has demonstrated its determination to raise interest rates when and if inflation should begin. The risks of owning U.S. money -- an inability to service debts and the risk of inflation – all are minimal.

If you owned a legal, money-printing press, would you ever go bankrupt? The government owns just such a printing press.

**Stop and Think:** The ability of U.S. government to borrow depends *partly* on its credit rating. What other factors determine the ability of anyone, including the government, to borrow? Do you believe these factors give the U.S. government the unlimited ability to borrow (create money) and the unlimited ability to pay its debts? Why or why not?

Why is it vital to the economic health of the world for the U.S. federal debt to increase faster than the U.S. rate of inflation?

## *Chapter 6. -- How Much Can the Government Borrow?*

*"Clinton, GOP hail budget, tax deal . . . would yield the first balanced budget since 1969"* Chicago Tribune, *May 3, 1997.*

*"For the nation's economy, it doesn't get much better than this."* Chicago Tribune, *May 3, 1997*

Three factors affect the ability of the government, to create money: Credit rating, comparative returns and availability of lending funds.

1) ***Credit rating:*** When there is no risk of default and no risk of inflation, a nation has a perfect credit rating. If the U.S. remains economically strong, its credit rating will remain virtually unlimited. Lenders consider it improbable that an economically strong U.S. would default on its debts.

The Federal Reserve Board maintains control over inflation, by raising interest rates at the slightest inflationary hint. Equally important, the Fed *makes it known* it will not tolerate inflation, thereby reassuring borrowers.

2) ***Comparative returns*** offered by U.S. Treasury debt compared to returns on all other investments. The U.S. government can cause or allow its interest rates to go as high as necessary to sell its debt.

Much U.S. debt is sold at auction, which allows the market to dictate the interest rate. If other forms of investment were to offer more attractive returns, the market would require the U.S. to pay higher rates of interest. There always will be some level of interest at which U.S. debt will be attractive.

Since 1970, the rate of interest paid for a U.S. Treasury bill has had a 400% range, from more than 13% to less than 3%.

3) ***Availability of lending funds***: Because borrowing *creates* money, the more the U.S. borrows, the more federal money becomes available to potential lenders.

Assume the federal government sells a T-bill for $1,000. The economy sends $1,000 in cash to the government and the government sends back a T-bill. The government also sends the $1,000 in cash back into the economy to pay for goods, services and entitlements.

Now the economy, once again has $1,000 with which to buy another T-bill. The whole process can be repeated again and again, with the same $1,000 in cash buying endless T-bills.

**What Is the Circular, Illogical, Yet Indispensable Reasoning That Supports the World's Economies?**

1) The "full faith and credit" of the U.S. is a desirable collateral for backing U.S. money.
2) Why is it desirable? The U.S. economy is strong, and the U.S. has demonstrated the ability and willingness to service debts and to prevent inflation.
3) What makes our economy strong? We have created money to support a large and growing production and purchasing base, and to pay our debts.
4) Why are we able to create money? The "full faith and credit" of the U.S. is desirable.

The value of money is based on this tacit agreement among all nations: Products having intrinsic value can be exchanged for money, which has no intrinsic value.

Why would any merchant give you food, clothing, machinery and all manner of goods and services in exchange for intrinsically worthless pieces of paper?

Because without such agreement, the world would grind to a stop. It is not possible to create, store, evaluate and transport physical goods in sufficient quantity to support the world's trading needs.

**Why Not Rely on Gold?**

**Stop and Think:** Why is balanced federal budget identical with being on the gold standard?

Prior to 1821, when Great Britain went on a gold standard, silver was the world's principal monetary metal. For fifty years following 1821, both gold and silver were used as money.

In the 1870's, Germany, France, the U.S. and other countries adopted a gold standard, because gold discoveries in the western states made gold more available. That began the worldwide gold standard, which lasted until 1914.

From 1914 until 1928, shortages of gold and difficulty of transportation (during World War I) caused the world to resort to paper money. In 1928, gold was reestablished, except not in a gold standard but in a "gold-exchange" standard. Gold reserves were supplemented with currency that was convertible to gold at a fixed rate of exchange.

The gold-exchange standard disappeared during the Great Depression, proving once again that gold could be used as money, so long as nothing went wrong. As soon as there were troubles (war, depression, shortages) gold had to be abandoned.

The irony is that gold was adopted to prevent economic dislocations, but its scarcity and difficulty of handling forced the very problem it was supposed to prevent.

The main purpose of a gold standard is to restrict the ability of a government to create money, which was felt to be inflationary. In this sense, a gold standard is identical to a balanced federal budget.

Following World War II, gold was given a fixed price of $35 an ounce. When the U.S. predictably ran short of gold, President Nixon allowed the U.S. dollar to "float" against the price of gold and other currencies. It was another way of saying we were off any type of gold standard. This act saved the world's economies.

The U.S. abandoned gold to control the amount of U.S. government money in circulation, and to control the value of that money (inflation). Gold does not allow a government to manage its supply of money, because the supply of newly-mined gold bears no relationship to money needs.

Being locked to gold means being locked to the economies of all other countries. It causes nations to fall like dominos when one large nation suffers a recession. That is how gold-based America exported its depression to the world.

*Question:* If gold is not money, why do we continue to maintain large stocks of gold?

*Answer:* We also maintain large inventories of cheese, butter, oil, obsolete bullets for obsolete guns and many other items. There is no more reason to maintain a stock of gold than there is to maintain a stock of any other commodity that might be bartered or used in industry.

People who believe there is safety in gold, have paid a terrible price. Gold has lost all standing as a hedge against inflation. In the past 20 years, the price of gold has fallen faster than the value of paper money. In 1980, gold rose into the $800 range. As this is written, it is well below $400.

Paper money held its value twice as well as gold. Further, gold doesn't pay interest and it is expensive to store.

Being on the gold standard put us in financial trouble, because it limited our money-creation ability. Not having learned from that crisis, the politicians again want to limit our money-creation ability by mandating a surplus.

**What Will Happen When Our Debt Increases Less Than Our Inflation Rate?**

**Stop and Think:** Visualize inflation at, for instance, 3%, while the total debt grows 2% a year. Is this bad or good? Visualize the figures reversed: Inflation is 2% and total debt grows 3% a year. Is *this* bad or good? Why?

A growing U.S. debt increases the number of dollars in the world. Inflation decreases the purchasing value of each dollar. So long as the total number of dollars grows faster than the U.S. inflation rate the world is enriched.

The simple formula is:

*Total number of dollars x purchasing value of each dollar = Total value of dollars.*

Assume that in 1983 you had $1 thousand, and you assigned the purchasing value of $1.00 to each dollar. The real value of your money would have been $1,000. ($1,000 x $1.00).

Ten years pass, and your holdings double to $2 thousand. Because of inflation, the purchasing value of each dollar is only .69. Now your money would be worth $1,380 ($2,000 x .69) in constant dollars.

You have more real money because your total number of dollars increased faster than inflation. The *amount* of your money increased faster than the decrease in the *value* of each dollar.

If your total dollars had increased by only 25% to $1,250, your money would be worth only $862.50 in constant terms. You would have lost real money.

When the U.S. inflation rate exceeds the growth of U.S. dollars, the total real value of U.S. money in America and the world declines, and America and the world are impoverished.

This may be one of the least understood principles in all of economics:

> *The economic health of America and the world requires that U.S. total debt grow faster than U.S. inflation.*

> **Stop and Think:** What causes inflation? Finish this sentence: "Inflation occurs when there is too much money relative to ________________."

## *Chapter 7. -- What Causes Inflation?*

*"The debate over the CPI was reignited last December when a presidential commission . . . estimated the overstatement (of inflation) to be as high as 1.1 percent." Pat Widder,* Chicago Tribune, *April 23, 1997.*

*"Robust economic conditions . . . over the past few years typically signal higher inflation. However . . . inflation is lower now than it was in 1994 . . . Whatever the reason, the recent weakness of inflation raises an uncertainty as to how to interpret conventional measures of inflationary pressures." September 1997,* The Economic Outlook, *Congressional Budget Office*

We all know inflation is "when prices go up." More precisely:

| *Inflation is money's loss of value when compared to the average value of goods and services.* |
|---|

If the price of milk goes from one dollar to two dollars, what has happened? Either the value of a dollar has gone down, the value of milk has gone up, or both.

The person, who wishes to trade milk for dollars, has changed his attitude about the relative values of dollars and milk. He now demands more dollars in exchange for milk. The person who wishes to trade dollars for milk, now must offer more dollars for the milk.

Inflation does not result from the increase in value of one product. To measure inflation, the government averages the values of many products in many geographic areas, and even this is inadequate.

Inflation is the average increase in dollar cost of all the products sold everywhere in our economy.

**Measuring Inflation – Nobody Can Do It**

It is impossible to measure this change. Inflation does not affect all people or products equally.

If the average price of breakfast cereal were to rise, those families who buy the most breakfast cereal would be most affected. If you bought no breakfast cereal, you would say, "What inflation?"

Products come into existence, change and disappear. How has the price of television sets changed during the past twenty years?

You might ask, "What kind of television sets? Black and white, or color? Floor models or table models? Twenty inch or forty inch? Remote control? Multiple picture? Cable-ready? DVD? Flat screen? Etc."

You also might ask, "How will we weigh the most frequently purchased sets vs. the less frequently purchased, since this has changed through time?"

What has been the change in price of eight-track tape players? The answer will not help you measure inflation. Eight-track tape players are obsolete, and no longer sold. If they once were included in the measure of average prices, what would you now include?

Another problem: Averaging. If the average price (whatever that is) of long distance calls has dropped 20% and the average price of milk has risen 10%, what has been the inflation? How would you factor together the price changes in thousands of products to develop one inflation figure?

Trying to determine the "inflation" for even one product can be tricky. Now multiply one product by the millions of products we buy, and you see why the measure of inflation is subjective.

In 1997, the Bureau of Labor Statistics began an experiment, attempting to estimate inflation by recalculating price changes in only 207 items in just forty-four geographic areas.

In 2000, the Federal Reserve Board told Congress, the approved measure of inflation has overestimated "real" inflation, and should be changed.

Since Congress long has been aware of the inflation measure's shortcomings, why the sudden discovery? Because lowering the official inflation rate reduces the government's obligation to increase Social Security benefits.

This is felt to be good, by those who enjoy a federal surplus. It is bad for retired people. Budget balancers profess concern about future generations, but seem unconcerned about current generations.

(My guarantee: Congress will "discover" this latest measure is wrong, and search for a new one.)

Certain products and services have not changed much through the years, for example, unprocessed food products and unskilled labor. The prices of these basic products and services have tended to inflate. So whether or not inflation is measured with scientific accuracy, it is clear that today more dollars are needed to exchange for most goods and services.

Inflation is money's loss of value compared to the values of goods and services. So, has the value of money gone down or have the average values of goods and services gone up?

Years ago, an unskilled laborer might trade a full day's work for five dollars. Today, the minimum *hourly* wage exceeds five dollars, and an unskilled laborer would expect well more than forty dollars for an eight-hour day. Has the value of the man's labor increased or has the value of money decreased?

If you were to ask the same kinds of questions about every product or service in existence, you would find that the value of a dollar has gone down.

True, many products are more sophisticated, more useful or just plain better than were comparable products of years ago. But, I believe inflation is caused more by the loss in value of money than by the gain in value of goods and services.

**Common -- And Wrong -- Theories About the Causes of Inflation**

One theory dates from at least the 18th century (David Hume). It continued to be popular into the 1950's. It said, inflation is determined by the *quantity of money* in the economy. The belief was that adding money to the economy caused inflation. (In this case, the definition of "money" is limited to currency and coins, which in itself is a serious weakness.)

Many people continue to believe some form of this theory. That is one of several reasons put forth to reduce the federal debt.

John M. Keynes felt there is a predictable gap between increases in consumers' income and consumption expenditures. He felt inflation is caused by consumer and government attempts to buy more goods and services than our economy can supply.

This is the familiar, though false, concept that "inflation is *too many dollars chasing too few goods and services.*"

"Too many dollars" means "too much demand." However, for the vast majority of products and services in our economy, supply accommodates to demand, and in fact, often overcompensates.

If the demand for cheese were to rise, the price of cheese would rise. In response, farmers would produce more cheese, which would push prices back down.

If the farmers and manufacturers miscalculated and produced too much cheese, the price could drop below its starting point -- an effect that occurs frequently with agricultural products.

The degree to which supply, price and demand respond to each other is called "elasticity." The more necessary to life a product is, the less demand elasticity it has. If the price of heating oil doubled, the demand would not drop proportionately. The demand for heating oil is relatively inelastic.

A third theory holds that price increases are caused by *increases in production costs*. Increased mechanization and computerization have increased production efficiency. So, production cost increases come primarily from increased wage costs, leading to the notorious, though fictional, "wage-price spiral."

(The concept is, increased wages cause production costs to rise, causing prices to rise, causing workers to demand higher wages.)

One weakness of this theory is, workers always demand as much income as they think they can get, regardless of inflation. Price rises do not cause workers' salary demands to become more intense or more effective.

A second weakness is, manufacturers always charge as much as they think they can, to maximize total profits. There are businesses with 2 percent markups and businesses with 500 percent markups. In each case, the manufacturer charges as much as he can, competition and demand allowing, regardless of costs.

Higher production costs do not necessarily lead to higher selling prices. They also can lead to lower profits, fewer producers, substitute products, increased mechanization (when labor costs rise), greater efficiency -- any number of effects.

*The wage-price spiral is a fiction.*

All these theories and their brothers and cousins are correct in the short run for individual products, and all are defective over the longer run for the economy as a whole.

Even the federal government is confused about what causes inflation, as demonstrated by this quote from the Congressional Budget Office Outlook, September 1997:

> "The benign behavior of inflation over the past year is puzzling. Conventional measures of inflationary pressures from both the product and labor markets suggested an increase in the underlying rate of inflation in late 1996 or 1997.
>
> "Several temporary masking factors may account for much of the 'missing inflation.' Alternatively, some analysts suggest that the economy has changed in a way that makes inflation less responsive to pressures from a buildup of demand.
>
> "Unfortunately, uncertainty surrounds both measures of demand pressures and the estimated size and timing of the inflationary response to those pressures. As a result, determining the precise reason why inflation has been so subdued is extremely difficult."

This is government-speak for, "We don't want you to know we have no idea what's happening."

**The True Cause of Inflation – Surprised?**

Money is a commodity, like gasoline, lumber, corn or milk. The value of any commodity depends on the supply and the demand for that commodity. If the supply of milk grows faster than the demand for milk, the price (dollar value) of milk falls.

> **Stop and Think:** Imagine you live on a remote island. Grains of wheat are money, and one hundred grains of wheat can buy one gallon of gasoline. If, after time, two hundred grains of wheat are required, you would call that "inflation." What factors could cause the price of gasoline to rise from one hundred grains of wheat to two hundred grains?

Inflation occurs when the supply of a country's money grows faster than the demand for that country's money, compared with the supply and demand for goods and services.

The formulas are:

**DG/SG = VG** and **DM/SM = VM**

D=Demand; S=Supply; V=Value; G=Goods and Services; M=Money, I=Inflation

To get to the formula for inflation, plug in the formulas for the values of money and goods/services:

**(DG / SG) / (DM / SM) = I**

which simplifies to:

**VG/VM = I**

The higher the value of goods, or the lower the value of money, the higher will be inflation.

Inflation is the ratio of two ratios: The supply and demand for goods and services, and the supply and demand for money. *Mathematically*, both numbers in the VG/VM fraction are equally meaningful. Changes in either number affect world inflation. But the realities are much different.

Air is in great demand, because we all must breathe it, but the supply is ample, so air has little or no commercial value. Supply outweighs demand so the price is low.

Rabid dogs are in low supply, but the demand for them is limited, so rabid dogs have no commercial value. Again, supply outweighs demand, and again, the price is low.

Many countries have had strong currencies, later to see the value of their currencies weaken. The most severe drop in the value of a country's money is known as "hyperinflation."

Borrowing creates money, and inflation continues (erroneously) to be defined as "too much money relative to the supply of goods and services." Yet while you have seen the U.S. federal debt increase dramatically in 1980s and 1990s, U.S. inflation has remained at an acceptably "low" level.

This constitutes absolute proof that increasing federal debt does not cause inflation – a proof ignored by those who expound on the inflationary dangers of federal debt.

Return to our equations for inflation:

**DG/SG = VG** and **DM/SM = VM.**

And **VG/VM = I.**

The formulas show, if the demand for goods and services goes up, their value goes up. If the demand for money goes up, the value of money goes up. And if the value of goods goes up faster than the value of money, you have inflation.

However, **DG/SG** works much differently from **DM/SM**. First, the DG is a compilation of the demands for all goods and services. It never rises as a unit. The demand for some goods and services rises while the demand for others falls.

Second, an increase in the supply of goods reduces prices which increases demand. This increase in demand modifies the price decrease and may actually raise prices over time (because new buying habits are formed). This is why producers distribute free samples and coupons.

A decrease in the supply of goods raises prices and causes a decrease in demand. This may bring prices to below prior levels (because of production efficiencies.)

**DG/SG** tends to move slowly and be at least partially self-leveling and market dominated. *The market* responds to price changes by adjusting both supply and demand.

This cannot be said of **DM/SM.** Though money comes in many varieties, all varieties of money (in any one country) tend to move together. In this discussion, money can be considered a single product.

The ratio between the total supply and demand for money is partly market-dominated *and partly government-dominated.* The government may increase the supply of money by selling Treasury bonds, notes and bills.

Given this information, one might expect the increase in supply to reduce the price (interest rate) of money. However, the opposite can happen. To sell a large supply of bonds, the government might need to demand by *paying a higher price for money* (higher interest rates). This happens only in the very short term, however.

While the government has limited control over the supply and demand for all goods and services (through its own purchases), it has more control over the supply and demand for money.

The government controls supply when it creates and destroys money, and the government controls demand when it adjusts interest rates. Because of extensive government intervention, the value of money tends to be more controlled than self-leveling.

On balance, the government's creation of money is related more to the government's need for money than to inflation considerations. The government's primary anti-inflation tool is its control over the price of money (interest rates), which affects the demand for money.

Inflation is not “too much money relative to the supply of goods and services.” Given enough money for production and purchasing, the supply of goods and services has and will continue to increase endlessly, to satisfy infinite human desires.

In all of human history, there never has been an economy that had too much money relative to the supply of goods and services -- not prewar Germany, not Brazil, not China, not any of the inflation-afflicted economies.

If the supply of money increases more than the demand for money, there will be inflation. Insufficient demand is not caused by the absence of things to buy; it is caused by the insufficient reward, when compared with the risk of owning money.

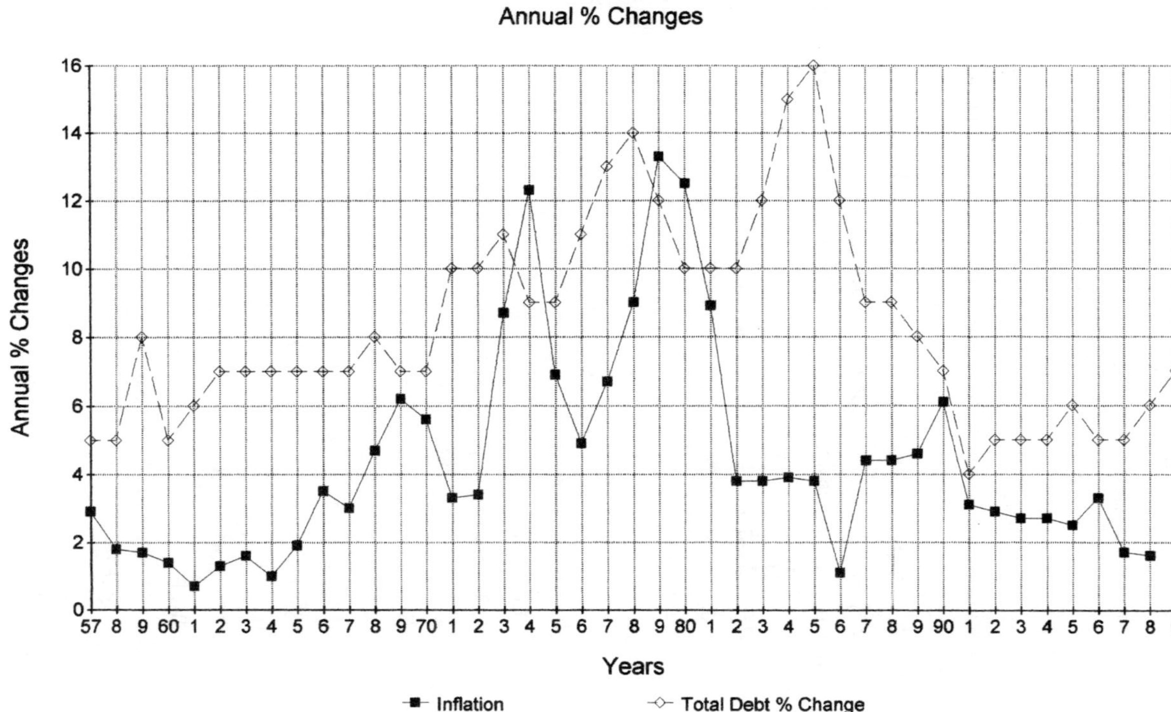
Debt v. Inflation
Annual % Changes
Annual % Changes
16
14
12
10
8
6
4
2
0
57 8 9 60 1 2 3 4 5 6 7 8 9 70 1 2 3 4 5 6 7 8 9 80 1 2 3 4 5 6 7 8 9 90 1 2 3 4 5 6 7 8 9
Years
Inflation
Total Debt % Change

**Government Control of Inflation**

Governments can control the value of money through gross measures such as devaluation (reduction of value) or the rarely considered, revaluation (increase in value). Devaluation means the government pays more units of its money for units of other countries' moneys. Many governments have devalued their currencies, trying to encourage exports.

The effect is instant inflation, because the nation must pay more for imported goods. A money devaluation of 50 percent will cause an immediate inflation of about 100 percent, for imported goods.

As our economy becomes more a part of a world economy, the supply and demand for goods and services will continue to have less impact on any one nation's inflation. If the supply of domestic products drops, imported products will fill the gap. If the supply of labor drops, goods will be produced overseas.

In the VG/VM relationship (value of goods/ value of money), VM is far more important to inflation.

The federal government exerts modest control over the supply and demand for goods and services. Though the government does order certain kinds of products produced -- for war, infrastructure, health care, etc. -- and other kinds of products purchased (corn, milk, etc.) a great deal of time elapses before a government project goes from discussions in Washington, D.C. to actual fruition of the project. Government manipulation of the VG factor provides a ponderous, and therefore, inadequate control over inflation.

Though a country may control the prices of goods, either by open market operations (for example, the U.S. government's buying of vast, unusable quantities of cheese) or by fiat (for example, President Nixon's price controls), such attempts always injure our economy, and at last, seem to be growing out of favor.

When Germany, Brazil and other countries experienced hyperinflation, the reason was not that there was too little available to buy or too little the people wanted to buy. Initially, there was much to buy and the people wanted to buy it.

The problem was that the world -- including the citizens of the countries themselves -- did not want to own the German or Brazilian monies. The reward (interest) was too low compared with the risk that these currencies would devalue in the future. When demand for the money fell, the price (value) of the money fell. That was inflation.

*On the surface, inflation is too large a supply of money relative to the demand for money. Bottom line: Inflation is caused by interest rates that are too low.*

**Steps Government Can Take**

There are two good steps any country can take to cure or to prevent inflation, and both steps boil down to the same thing:

1) Increase the demand for your money by raising interest rates.
2) Increase the demand for your money by reducing the risk your currency will be devalued. You must demonstrate your *willingness and determination* to prevent inflation by raising interest rates.

There also is one bad way a country can cure or prevent inflation. It can increase the value of its money by decreasing the supply. This will cause a depression. The cure would be worse than the disease.

The U.S. Federal Reserve Board has demonstrated its determination to prevent inflation from rising to above 3 percent. The world feels the risk of inflation in America is reduced to that level.

This belief allows the Federal Reserve to control inflation with lower interest rates than if the world were less confident about

America's potential for inflation. If the Federal Reserve vacillated in its determination, interest rates would need to be higher, just to maintain the demand by a world nervous about risk.

*The* willingness *to raise interest rates reduces the* need *to raise interest rates.*

**To a Hammer, Every Problem is a Nail.**

The Federal Reserve has one major tool: interest rate control. It attempts to use that tool to solve all economic problems. Recently the Fed used its tool for the wrong problem. It believed inflation came from an "overheated" economy, an economy that grows "too fast."

When the Fed detected our economy growing above its arbitrary target (about 2% a year), it raised interest rates, which prevented inflation by increasing the demand for money, but did nothing about the "heat" of the economy.

And what is "overheated"? The Fed has no idea, just some vague notion that if the economy grows "too fast" (?) this is cause for concern. Thus, the Chairman of the Fed pontificated about "irrational exuberance," and the nation nodded solemnly, as though some great Truth had been revealed.

There is no evidence a fast-growing economy is more inflation-prone than a slow-growing economy. Our "irrational exuberance" did not cause inflation. Those economies experiencing hyperinflation were not "overheated."

The economy just prior to the Great Depression wasn't overheated; it was under funded. "Irrational exuberance" is meaningless.

Most recently, Chairman Greenspan reduced interest rates in a desperate effort to prevent inflation. He will fail. The public will discover the emperor has no clothes.

## That Incurable "Stagflation" And How to Cure It

"Stagflation" is a stagnant economy with inflation. This problem is the Fed's worst nightmare, because the Fed's one tool won't cure it. The traditional cure for economic stagnation, low interest rates, leads to inflation. And the cure for inflation (raising interest rates) is felt to cause economic stagnation (though it doesn't).

Inflation is the opposite of deflation, not recession, so the same tool used to cure inflation, can't be reversed to cure recession.

The existence of "stagflation" proves there is no relationship between inflation and economic growth. President Nixon faced stagflation and made the disastrous decision to freeze prices.

Hyperinflation most often occurs in countries having modest or even no economic growth. Further, the countries that had the greatest postwar economic growth, for example Japan and Germany, have not suffered from inflations unacceptable to their governments.

How can the government cure stagflation? Cure each of the two problems. A stagnant economy can be revived by pumping enough money into it. This increases both the supply of, and the demand for, goods and services, which increases productivity, jobs and purchasing. Poof! Stagnancy is gone.

Inflation can be cured by raising interest rates, which increases money's value. Increased interest rates also make federal money creation easier.

And, as we'll discuss later, rising interest rates do not stagnate our economy.

The Fed's anti-inflation policy of controlling the demand for money (via interest manipulation) works well, so long as the supply of money keeps growing. When total debt stops growing, a recession results. At that point, reducing interest rates causes stagflation. The Fed's tool is useless.

**Do Low Interest Rates Make Borrowing Easier?**

Money is the credit/debt twins. For every debt there is a lender and a borrower. Low interest rates make borrowing more attractive, but what about lending?

Would you buy a bond (lend) paying a low interest rate? Wouldn't you rather put your money into stocks or real estate, if all you could get for a bond investment were 2%? On the other side, would you like to issue a bond (borrow) if you had to pay 30%?

High rates encourage lending. Low rates encourage borrowing.

*Because there are two sides to every loan, neither low interest rates nor high interest rates affect the overall ease of private borrowing/lending.*

That is yet another blow to conventional wisdom. Low interest rates do not make borrowing easier, because they make lending less attractive.

One exception to this rule makes our prosperous economy possible. Find a borrower who doesn't care what interest rate he pays. Then, high interest rates will bring forth more lenders, which makes borrowing easier.

And who is this borrower who doesn't care what interest he pays? The federal government.

U.S. federal debt must compete for lenders with the debt of all other nations. The higher the domestic interest rates, the easier the borrowing.

*High interest rates make government borrowing easier.*

No matter how high the interest rates, the government borrows what it needs, neither more nor less. U.S. debt is considered a low risk investment, lower than land, gold, diamonds, stocks, municipal bonds, corporate bonds or most other nations' money, because the world believes:

1) The U.S. government will not default on its debts.
2) The Federal Reserve will not allow high inflation.

With risk already low, demand for U.S. credit/dollars may be stimulated with modest increases in interest rates. More people will want to buy Treasury bonds, notes and bills when interest rates are higher than when rates are lower.

The demand even for currency, a form of money that pays no interest, is stimulated by increasing interest rates. The Treasury sells U.S. Treasury bonds, notes and bills in exchange for U.S. money. A foreigner who wants to purchase U.S. federal debt, first must buy U.S. money from someone who exchanges money.

If U.S. currency were cheaper than other forms of U.S. money, buyers would gravitate to currency. The increased demand would raise currency's price.

Corporate bonds pay a higher interest rate than do U.S. bonds. Even the best corporations have poorer credit ratings than the U.S. government.

Prewar Germany, Brazil, et al, generated too little demand for their money. Had these countries acted quickly to raise interest rates, they would have avoided hyperinflation.

*For every level of risk, there is some level of reward that makes the risk worthwhile.*

Those who did not buy Brazilian money when the Brazilian government was paying 15%, would have bought it at a return of

50%. Or 150%. Or 5,000%. At some level, demand for Brazilian money would have been stimulated, and the hyperinflation would have ended.

Where would Brazil have found the money to pay those interest rates? By selling bonds, notes and bills, which would have been made possible by the high rates.

As demand for Brazilian money rose, confidence in the Brazilian monetary system and the Brazilian economy would have grown, and the Brazilian government would have been able lower interest rates. Inflation would have been defeated.

During the fastest federal debt increase in our history, inflation remained low -- proof that a large federal debt need not be inflationary. Inflation can be prevented or cured by setting interest rates high enough to generate sufficient demand for credit/dollars.

Year after year "debt hawks" tell us a high federal debt will cause inflation. Year after year they were proved wrong. You receive more accurate predictions from the local palm reader.

Consider the pitiful case of Henry Figgie, Jr., the wealthy author of a 1993 book titled, *Bankruptcy 1995*. Based on our increasing national debt Figgie predicted we would suffer massive inflation, the loss of our property to foreigners and, of course, bankruptcy.

The only thing approaching bankruptcy was Figgie International, which acted upon its boss's beliefs.

Do these spectacular failures deter the debt hawks? In November 1996, Morton Kaplan, publisher of *The World and I* magazine, referred to America as "A nation barreling toward bankruptcy (because of) the fiscal burden of entitlement programs like Social Security and Medicare."

Year after year, we have been "barreling" and year after year Mr. Kaplan and his experts worried, while our healthy economy kept growing.

Does it surprise you that a brilliant expert from the University of Chicago (America's premier producer of Nobel prizes), cannot see the plain facts before him? It shouldn't, if you understand the power of cognitive dissonance.

**Does Unemployment Affect Inflation?**

The theory: When unemployment is low, business must pay higher wages to scarce workers. Higher labor costs cause higher production costs, which lead to higher prices.

In 1994, unemployment was above 6.5%. By 1996 it had fallen more than 15% to below 5.5%, which seems to imply that wages must rise, causing inflation. Inflation remained low.

| *Low unemployment does not cause inflation .* |
|---|

To quote from the March 3, 1997 Chicago Tribune: "The unemployment rate hit a 23-year low as the number of jobs grows, but inflation doesn't."

By November, 2000, unemployment "reached its lowest point since 1969" (*Time Magazine*, January 8, 2000), and inflation remained low.

We are in a world economy, and the U.S. economy is influenced by world events. Imports, exports, the value of money in all other countries, worldwide production, weather, wars, politics etc., affect our inflation rate more than does our domestic unemployment.

Inflation describes the *relationship* between the value of money and the value of goods. The fact that the cost of producing goods goes up, does not mean the price of these goods must go up. If there is insufficient demand at a higher price, the price will come down, and manufacturers will settle for lower margins.

When the value of money goes up, the price of goods comes down. Those shoppers who traveled to Europe in the early 1980's came home with bargains, not because the cost of producing European goods had gone down, but because the value of the American dollar was high.

Experts have difficulty predicting effect from cause in our economy. It is complicated and any single factor will be overwhelmed by the myriad other factors. Using unemployment to predict inflation is like predicting this year's weather based on the "greenhouse gas" emissions from one car.

*Inflation is less product-driven than money-driven.*

*"In fact, every time – at least since World War II – the Fed has tried to slow the economy by inducing unemployment increases of more than three-tenths of a percentage point, it has produced a recession.* Chicago Tribune, June 25, 2000.

Reduced unemployment has not caused the inflation that experts at the Federal Reserve Board thought it must. (The Fed continues to use unemployment as a strong predictive factor for inflation – another example of cognitive dissonance.)

Of the four factors affecting inflation – risk and reward (for money), and desire and scarcity (for products and services) -- the most significant in terms of the U.S. economy, and also the most controllable, is *money reward.*

On a micro scale, owning one form of money can have high risk. An individual corporation that has issued bonds can go bankrupt overnight.

But on a macro scale, the risk of default for all U.S. money in total, changes very slowly if at all. It is the reward that can change without notice. The Federal Reserve, which controls interest rates, never gives notice of its plans.

*U.S. inflation is determined by the value of U.S. money, which is driven by the demand for money, which is driven by interest rates.*

Preventing inflation requires us to maintain sufficient demand for U.S. dollars. Since our credit rating scarcely can be improved from its near-perfect level, the best way to maintain demand is to make sure interest rates are sufficiently high.

## *Chapter 8. -- Is the Savings Rate in America Too Low?*

The widespread belief is, if we imprudent, spoiled, live-for-today Americans would save more, we would be able to afford the important things in life like homes, college educations, pensions and quality health care.

The fact that we are the most prolific home-owning, college-attending, pension-creating, quality-health-care-receiving people on earth, does not influence the experts, who try to make us feel guilty about being wastrels. We have accomplished what experts say we cannot accomplish.

Comparisons are made with the savings rates in other countries, and Americans always seem to be big spenders and indifferent savers. For example, the savings rate in Japan traditionally was about four times the rate in America. Whether that translated into a better standard of living for the Japanese is questionable.

In 1992, the government said personal savings as a percentage of disposable personal income was more than 9%. In year 2000, it dropped below zero. ("Spending has risen more than income, and saving reached a record low." *Time Magazine*, January 8, 2001.) This decline in savings came during the economic boom of the 1990's.

**Stop and Think**: What is the difference between saving and spending? List activities you consider "saving" and those you consider "spending."

What is the difference between saving and *lending*? List examples of saving that are lending and examples of saving that are not lending.

**What Is "Saving," And What Is "Spending?"**

Although the word "save" seems to have a more prudent cachet than "spend," and certainly more than "borrow," few people know the real difference.

According to the U.S. Bureau of Economic Analysis, *National Income and Product Accounts of the United States*, Gross Saving includes such items as: personal saving, undistributed corporate profits (less adjustments for inventory), corporate consumption of fixed capital, non corporate consumption of fixed capital, less federal, state and local deficits. Understand?

Because Gross Saving includes so many items, a case can be made that the savings rate is too low, too high or just right, depending on which items you include and which logic you employ. Through the past twenty years, while our economy has grown massively, the level of that thing called "personal saving" hardly has changed, remaining in the range of $150 billion to $200 billion.

Since "personal saving" has declined as a percentage of our economy, this could be seen as "bad," by those who advocate saving. In contrast, "undistributed corporate profits" as a part of Gross Saving, has risen. Is this good or bad?

The reason "undistributed corporate profits" rose so much is because the inventory valuation adjustment and capital consumption adjustment both fell. So is *this* good or bad?

Before you answer, let me assure you there is no answer. You can perform an analysis by dividing each of the above variables into smaller variables, ad infinitum. You then will have developed enough mini variables to be able to put whatever spin you wish on the larger figures, and "prove" we either are teetering on the brink of disaster, tapping at the door of Utopia, or tottering anywhere in between.

Rather than engage in the sophistry of minutia, try to examine the bigger picture -- what most people would consider the plain meaning of the question, "Should Americans save more?"

Here is a short list. Decide which activities you consider "saving." Develop your own rules about what is "saving."

Do you "save" when you:

1. Bury your currency in a tin can in your back yard?
2. Deposit your money in your bank savings account or in your money market account?
3. Purchase Treasury bills or bank CDs?
4. Purchase guaranteed-interest, whole life insurance?
5. Purchase stocks and bonds?
6. Purchase real estate?
7. Purchase a business?
8. Purchase your primary residence?
9. Purchase a secondary residence?
10. Purchase a car for your business use?
11. Purchase a car for your personal use?
12. Purchase a television set?
13. Purchase food and clothing?

Saving and spending both involve a transfer of money. Most people would consider items #1 - #5 to be forms of saving.

(The U.S. Department of Education lists under "*Savings Instruments*": "savings accounts," "CDs," "money market accounts and money market mutual funds" and "U.S. savings bonds." It lists as "*Investments*": "mutual funds," "corporate stocks and bonds" and "U.S. treasury securities." Do you agree?)

Did items #6-8 make your list? If you feel paying down your mortgage is a form of saving, would the actual purchase of your home -- that is, making the down payment -- be the start of saving?

How different is the purchase of a home, from the purchase of stocks and bonds? Purchasing a home is purchasing real estate. For many people, the purchase of a home is one of the best saving programs possible.

Item #9 (purchase a secondary residence) is a real estate transaction. Should your answer depend on whether you intend the secondary residence solely for personal use or to rent it out? That is, if it is to be used as an investment (as are Treasury bills and bank CDs), do you feel that's a form of saving?

Item #10 (purchase car for business) slides even farther away from "saving," though purchasing a car for business is not much different from purchasing a business that owns a car, which in itself is identical to buying stocks. Either way, you become a shareholder.

Most people consider item #11 (purchase a car for personal use) to be spending, though it is almost identical with item #10. The vast majority would consider purchasing a television set to be spending. But, what if your television set were located in your business? Does your use of an item determine whether that item is saving or spending?

And I imagine you called #13 (purchase food and clothing) to be spending – unless you sell food or clothing, in which case it's a business investment.

Can you determine where saving ends and investment and spending begin? Is there a meaningful difference between saving and investing? The government has made arbitrary selections that may not reflect the realities of our economy.

The most important forms of saving involve purchasing credit. When we buy Treasury bonds, notes and bills and corporate bonds, we require the government and the corporations to sell bonds, notes and bills. The more saving you do, the more credit you must purchase.

*If we are to save more, the government and/or private industry must borrow more.*

Saving and borrowing are the same act, as seen from two sides of the transaction. The same people who think America saves too little, also think America borrows too much. Cognitive dissonance.

**What Happens When Americans Save?**

To determine whether saving benefits our economy, compare the relative effect of a dollar saved with a dollar spent.

You use your money in one of three ways:

* To invest in credit, which creates money.
* To invest in assets such as land and stock, which creates no money, and merely exchanges the money and the assets between owners.
* To invest in depreciables and consumables, such as cars, food and clothing, which moves money from one owner to another.

**Stop and Think:** Which benefits the overall economy more, the purchase of a bond, the purchase of stock or the purchase of a car? Why?

When money is invested in credit (bonds, bills, notes, bank accounts, etc.), money is created and our economy becomes wealthier. To acquire a good quality of life, you buy depreciable assets like cars, and consumables like food and clothing. But a healthy, growing economy must invest in money-creating, credit investments.

*When the experts say we should save more, they mean we should lend more.*

Although home and auto sales are used as barometers of economic health, these purchases create no money. They circulate existing money. If you spend $20 thousand on a car, the car manufacturer and its workers and suppliers become $20 thousand wealthier.

You become poorer. You have “lost” your $20 thousand, and when you take possession of your car, it loses value. You lose money and you lose wealth.

Manufacturing the car creates wealth – a car is worth more than the value of the metal, plastic and rubber from which it is created. Selling the car reduces wealth, because the used car has less value than the new car. Through the entire transaction, wealth fluctuates, but the supply of money does not change.

If you open a 401(k) retirement plan, and use the plan money to purchase corporate stock, that would be considered saving. But too much purchasing of stock, and too little money creation, can leave our economy at risk, as occurred prior to the Great Depression.

The two years just preceding the Great Depression (1927-28) saw an enormous run-up in the price of stocks as people saved furiously. But stocks are not money and people did not want money; they wanted stock. Too little money was being created, and too little demand for money was created, so our economy suffered from the lack of money.

The balanced-budget people cannot explain how this country could emerge from a recession, if the government did not create additional money. They cannot explain, because there is no way.

*A balanced federal budget makes recessions or depressions likely to occur and impossible to cure.*

## *Chapter 9. -- Where Should the Government Spend Money?*

*"Any truly optimistic scenario for the future of the American economy involves substantially reducing the deficit . . ." Nicholas Lemann,* The Washington Monthly, *March 1993.*

*"It is a dream economy," Astrid Adolfson,* Chicago Tribune, *May 3, 1997*

We have seen that:

1. Without debt, there is no credit. All money is credit.
2. To grow, an economy needs the money supply to grow.
3. The true money supply includes bonds of all maturity lengths and of all debtors.
4. The safest and economically most beneficial forms of saving are credit.
5. Taxation destroys money, because it destroys credit.
6. Our government's credit rating is based on its ability and its willingness to pay and to fight inflation.
7. The U.S. can create money without limit, and can do so with modest interest rates, if it has an unlimited credit rating.
8. The reduced demand for money is inflation. The demand for money can be increased by increasing the reward for owning money (interest).
9. When the supply of U.S. money grows faster than inflation, the world is enriched. When the supply of U.S. money grows slower than inflation, the world is impoverished.
10. The government's deficit is the economy's surplus.

To free money, the U.S. government will reduce taxes and increase money creation, while adjusting interest rates to prevent inflation. This will cause the amount of money to grow more rapidly than inflation, so the *total value* of U.S. money will grow.

**Stop and Think:** What are the economic effects of *wasteful* spending by the government?

**The Effect of Wasteful Spending by The U.S. Government**

A "wasteful" expenditure is one that does not produce a value in proportion to the cost. To make unnecessary purchases and to overpay, are considered "wasteful."

The U.S. military's notorious $600 toilet seat became a symbol of government waste. Is wasteful spending harmful, neutral or helpful for our economy?

Assume the military spends $1 million buying bullets for obsolete guns. To pay for these useless bullets, the government sells $1 million worth of Treasury bonds.

The government sends its bonds into the financial markets, receives $1 million in return, then sends this $1 million to the bullet manufacturer. The government then classifies the bullets as "Top Secret," denies they exist and stores them in a hidden, underground location, where they never will be seen or heard of again -- until they poison the local water supply – which the government also will deny.

Whether or not the bullets ever are used, our economy has grown $1 million wealthier. The bond holders own $1 million worth of Treasury credit, and the bullet manufacturer receives a $1 million check.

The bullet manufacturer deposits $1 million into his bank account, which allows the bank to create more money by lending some of that $1 million to borrowers, who will put the money into their banks -- which will create even more money by lending it.

With each step, money is created, until the government's "waste" of $1 million adds about $10 million to our economy. That money is used for all typical purposes: salaries, investments, charity, infrastructure, etc. They all benefit.

Our economy would have benefitted more, had the government purchased something of economic value. This would have increased the *wealth* of our economy, not only by the $10 million of *money* but also by the economic value of the *goods or services*.

If the government levies taxes to pay for the bullets, the bullet manufacturer and his bank will continue to receive money, as though the government had borrowed.

But taxpayers must withdraw money from banks. The banks will be able to lend less to other people, who will be forced to withdraw money from their banks. Any economic benefit from the payment to the bullet maker will be offset by money taken from taxpayers.

> *All government spending, even "wasteful" spending," has a positive and multiplying effect on our economy. Taxation has a negative, multiplying effect on our economy.*

> **Stop and Think**: Which government expenditures would be most immediately beneficial to our economy? Make a list. Why do you feel this way?

**What are the Most Immediately Beneficial Government Expenditures?**

All government expenditures benefit our economy. The most immediately beneficial include, defense, ecosystem, infrastructure, research, medical services, education, law enforcement and welfare.

***Defense***: A strong army reduces the risk of attacks on our interests and the resultant economic costs. Because the American armed forces were able to beat back the Iraqi invasion of Kuwait, American interests in the Mideast were protected and strengthened. We stopped a dangerous aggressor, and we demonstrated to potential aggressors, the risk of attack on American interests.

The money the U.S. government spends on our military both enriches and protects our economy

After the Viet Nam war, and especially after the collapse of the Soviet Union, we have reduced the size of the U.S. military in favor of social spending. However, military spending does not take money from the poor or from anything else. Military spending adds money to our economy. It raises employment and lifts the income of all Americans, including the poor.

Military spending benefits people who have jobs in military production plants. It benefits people whose employers sell to military production plants and their workers. Military spending flows through society, benefitting everyone it touches.

Military spending is neither more nor less beneficial than social spending. Too little military spending risks our freedoms. Too little social spending risks our lives. Neither should be short-changed. The federal government should increase its expenditures for the military. This is a federal government obligation and a federal government capability.

***Infrastructure*** expenditures provide the foundation upon which a strong, growing economy is built, and they reduce the economic costs of bad roads, weak bridges, silted waterways, inadequate communications and transportation, etc. Infrastructure expenditures directly support a vast number of laborers, engineers, executives and entrepreneurs.

Much of our infrastructure has become aged. Many bridges languish in a dangerous or declining condition. Airports, roads, electrical and water supply and other elements need improvement. Our quality of life declines when our infrastructure deteriorates.

The federal government should increase direct expenditures on infrastructure considered national or interstate. The federal government should allocate money according to population, to the states and municipalities for infrastructure improvements that are considered local. The decisions regarding how this local money is spent should be left to the local government units.

***Ecosystem*** deterioration has an insidious effect on our lives. It often happens so slowly, we become accustomed to the latest insult.

Is the air 5% dirtier than it was ten years ago? Who can remember? Did we lose another species? Who can tell? There were hardly any of that species last year, anyway. Is the water too dirty for swimming? Well, the swimming hasn't been so good for quite a while.

Yet everything humans attempt during our short stay on earth is aimed toward improving our quality of life. If someone asks you what is the purpose of life, you might answer, "To survive well and to improve." And what is more important to our surviving well and improving than the quality, diversity and beauty of the world that surrounds us?

The things we do to deteriorate our ecosystem, involve money. Lumbermen are more concerned with money than with owls. Fishermen are more concerned with money than with whales. The individual car buyer and the individual car maker are more concerned with money than with clean air.

The real estate developer is more concerned with money than with wetlands. The manufacturer is more concerned with money than with acid rain.

Each feels the immediate effect of money. Each has large control over his money and only minuscule control over the environment.

If money is the motive for destruction, money can be the motive for preservation and reclamation. The government can establish incentives for not polluting, not destroying and not changing.

Years ago, the government began to pay farmers for not growing. That idea had the wrong goal (raising food prices), and even that goal was unclear and at odds with other government goals (preventing inflation).

But the program did yield one accidental benefit. Soil erosion and depletion were reduced. It was good for the land to go to grass. When the farmers replanted the land, it produced better.

If the government paid lumber companies to protect owls, fishermen not to whale, auto makers to develop non polluting cars, municipalities to clean their sewage better and factories to remove acid from their smoke, America could approach an Eden.

The federal government should increase expenditures for ecosystem problems that are considered national or interstate. The government should allocate money according to population, to the states and municipalities for ecosystem improvements that are considered local. The decisions regarding how this local money is spent should be left to the local government units.

***Research*** leads to advances in medicine, communication, ecological preservation, food production, transportation and our knowledge of the universe. Government funding helps support laboratories that also conduct private research. Many research groups cannot exist solely on private funding for private purposes.

Research seldom produces immediate results. During times when taxpayers and the government try to limit expenditures, the investments that yield the slowest outcome, are first to be cut. When we free money, there would be no need for cuts.

***Medical services*** reduce the social and economic costs associated with illness and old age. Providing care for the sick and elderly will allow many people to remain productive longer and allow others to require less care later.

Millions of Americans go without health insurance because of cost or availability. Current health or wealth need not be criteria for insurance protection. Social Security, Medicare, Medicaid and welfare must be protected and expanded.

***Education*** allows a country to maintain or improve its economic position. The most economically advanced countries also are the best educated. Since investments in education take years to pay off, immediate investment is necessary. The economic cost of ignorance is dependency and crime.

The best schools are where they receive the most funding. Years ago, my daughters attended one of the best high schools in America, New Trier High in Winnetka, Illinois.

Today it remains one of the best, partly because local residents spend a great deal of money to hire the best teachers and buy the best programs. Local pride and parental involvement are large factors, but it is easier to be proud and involved if money exists to support your efforts.

The federal government should allocate money to local governments for investment in the physical plants of elementary and high schools (which are in poor condition around the country), teachers, programs and administration. The federal government also should reward colleges that do the best job educating their students.

***Law enforcement*** reduces the economic and social costs of crime. The most immediate and effective way to cut crime is to increase the number of police.

Jane Byrne, a former mayor of Chicago, moved into Cabrini Green, a notorious, crime-ridden, housing project. She was surrounded by hundreds of police.

The crime rate at this hellish location dropped to zero. Later, when the mayor moved out and the police left, the crime rate rose again. For Mayor Byrne, it was an act of symbolism, and it taught a good, though perhaps unintended, lesson: The more and better police you have, the lower will be the crime rate. That is the single, best answer to the problem of crime.

Hiring more police, paying for better training, and buying them the most advanced communications, protection and detection tools would have an instant effect on crime, and it would provide jobs and add money to each local economy.

The federal government should allocate money to the states for support of state National Guards. These military units are the only entities that can act both as domestic police and as an international army. Under the command of each state governor they can provide a buffer against excessive power by the U.S. army. (Law changes would be required.)

Many expenditures that Congress often wants to reduce first -- defense, research, medical aid, ecology -- are the ones that should be increased first.

I recommend dividing the money among the federal, state and municipal governments to prevent an over-powerful federal government.

**Stop and Think:** Free Money eliminates federal taxes and increases federal spending. Why then, should people work? Why not have the government print currency, without limit, and give it to all the citizens? What would be the *specific* effect of such a policy?

***Welfare.*** Free Money does not require the government to *give* money to the people. It envisions the government *buying* goods and services. This would expand current, timid efforts to turn welfare into "workfare," and it would maintain the country's control over its resources.

Politicians can be oblivious to economic reality. President Clinton urged business to give jobs preferentially to people trying to get off welfare. Since efficient companies employ only the people they need, business would have to fire good workers to make room for welfare recipients. Or companies would have to hire unneeded or less qualified people.

Neither approach would benefit our economy. Even the President of the United States does not understand the economic world.

The federal government can and should create jobs for unemployed or welfare people, by supporting business. Government investments create jobs. Those unable to work because of medical problems, would be helped by improved medical care and improved supervision.

**Why Not Give Money to Everyone?**

If the government merely gave money to everyone, fewer Americans would work. A greater percentage of the goods and services would be imported and unemployment would fall for those people who did want to work.

If this scenario sounds familiar, it approximates the economy of Saudi Arabia. There, a large percentage of the population receives oil money with little or no labor. They employ foreigners to do the work. One danger of this situation lies in the power foreigners can begin to accumulate and the national weakness this causes

Having a foreign-dominated police and military would be precarious for any nation. Saudi Arabia, with all its money, is weak militarily and must depend on the U.S. for its safety.

Similarly, more U.S. people retire each year. The large population increase in retired people, who live on their own savings and/or government pensions, has helped the U.S. to keep the unemployment level low, and without inflation.

The U.S. has no experience with a much greater non working population. As the level of non employment (as opposed to "un"-employment, i.e., people looking for jobs) increases, more goods and services would need to be imported, unless productivity increased proportionately.

If productivity did not increase, there is a point at which the country would begin to lose control over its supply of resources. The danger would not be shortages, but rather control and power.

Saudi Arabia does not suffer from shortages, but from the insufficient power to control its resources. This loss of political, military, police and production power endangers Saudi Arabia.

Our working population is so huge, I believe the U.S. is decades away from the time when a too-small work force could endanger us. I also believe we will be saved by increases in productivity generated by investments in research.

Further, medical advances make working into an older age possible, likely and desirable. People may be reluctant to retire at sixty-five or even at a hundred. The potential "problem" of too small a work force may be self-correcting.

**Stop and Think:** The concept of "Free Money" is something you never have experienced before. Do you find it troubling? List the reasons you think Free Money will damage our economy.

**Seven Arguments Against Free Money**

I can imagine at seven reasons why people might believe the U.S. should not free money:

***Argument 1***: Free Money requires a huge increase in government borrowing. At some level, attracting additional bond buyers would require offering excessive interest rates. These high rates would inhibit consumer borrowing for homes, autos and even daily purchases. The high rates also would inhibit industrial borrowing for research, marketing, production and hiring.

***Response:*** A huge increase in government borrowing does not require offering "excessive" interest rates. Since borrowing creates money, a huge increase in borrowing would create a huge increase in funds available for further borrowing. Borrowing creates additional lenders. This could cause interest rates to fall, because more money would be chasing investments.

*In one year, from 1974 to 1975, federal debt rose nearly 20%. During the same year, the discount rate fell from 8% to 6%. From 1980 through 1986, federal debt rose between 10% and 20% every year. During that same period, the discount rate dropped from 13% to 6%.* Borrowing creates the money for further borrowing.

Federal debt needs only to offer high enough rates to attract investors. Since federal debt is safer than all other investments, the government can pay rates lower than investors receive elsewhere.

> **Stop and Think:** Many people feel high interest rates are bad for our economy. Do you agree? Why?

No one knows what "high" means. During and after World War II consumer interest rates often averaged below 3%, and our economy grew. These days, interest rates average almost three times as high, and still our economy grows.

Some experts fear that "high" interest rates restrict borrowing to purchase goods and services. (Note the confused irony in which lower individual debt is thought to be bad for business while lower government debt is thought to be good for our economy. Also note, these same experts believe consumers today borrow *too much*.)

With the short term exception of real estate and auto purchases, individual spending is not significantly affected by increases in interest rates. Credit card and personal loan rates average well above prime. Yet credit card borrowing is massive.

Even for real estate and cars, increased interest rates delay purchasing only in the short term, just as increased gasoline prices only temporarily reduce gas consumption.

From 1983 to 1996, between 509,000 and 756,000 new homes were sold each year. Prior to 1996, the best-selling year was 1986, when 750,000 homes were sold. That also was the year when mortgage rates averaged about 10%. The worst selling year was 1991, when mortgage rates averaged about 9%.

From 1988 to 1993, mortgage rates fell every year, yet new home sales also fell from 1988 to 1991, and though there was a recovery in 1992-1993, new home sales never reached their 1988 "high-interest" levels.

If you were to plot new home sales and interest rates on an annual graph, you would see no correlation. High interest rates do not hurt home sales.

Personal interest payments recirculate within our economy, so any negative effects are balanced by positive. Borrowers pay more; lenders receive more. Both are part of the same economy. Changes in interest rates do not affect the total amount of money in our economy (except for the minority of interest which is paid to foreign investors.)

There also has been the belief that high interest rates hurt our economy by making business borrowing more expensive. Yet, an increase in business interest accounts for a minuscule fraction of business expenses. Interest is paid from a company to a creditor, both within our economy, with no net effect on the total money supply.

The belief that raising interest rates hurts our economy, may be caused by short-term stock market effects. After higher interest rates are announced, or even the hint that interest rates *might* rise, the stock market briefly falls. The fall is caused by the knowledge that the market *always* falls when interest rates go up, so investors try to get out in advance -- a self-fulfilling prophesy.

This phenomenon is carried to ridiculous extremes these days, when *good* economic news causes the stock market to fall, because investors know good news is will cause the Federal Reserve Board to raise rates. Yet, good economic news will be reflected in higher business profits, which eventually will force stock prices higher.

In October of 1992, when we still were early in the most recent economic boom, interest rates had fallen to below 3%. As this is being written, rates are much higher.

The graph on the following page (GDP % Changes V. Discount Rates) shows that large increases in GDP seem to correspond more closely with higher interest rates. History proves that high interest rates do not adversely affect the economy.

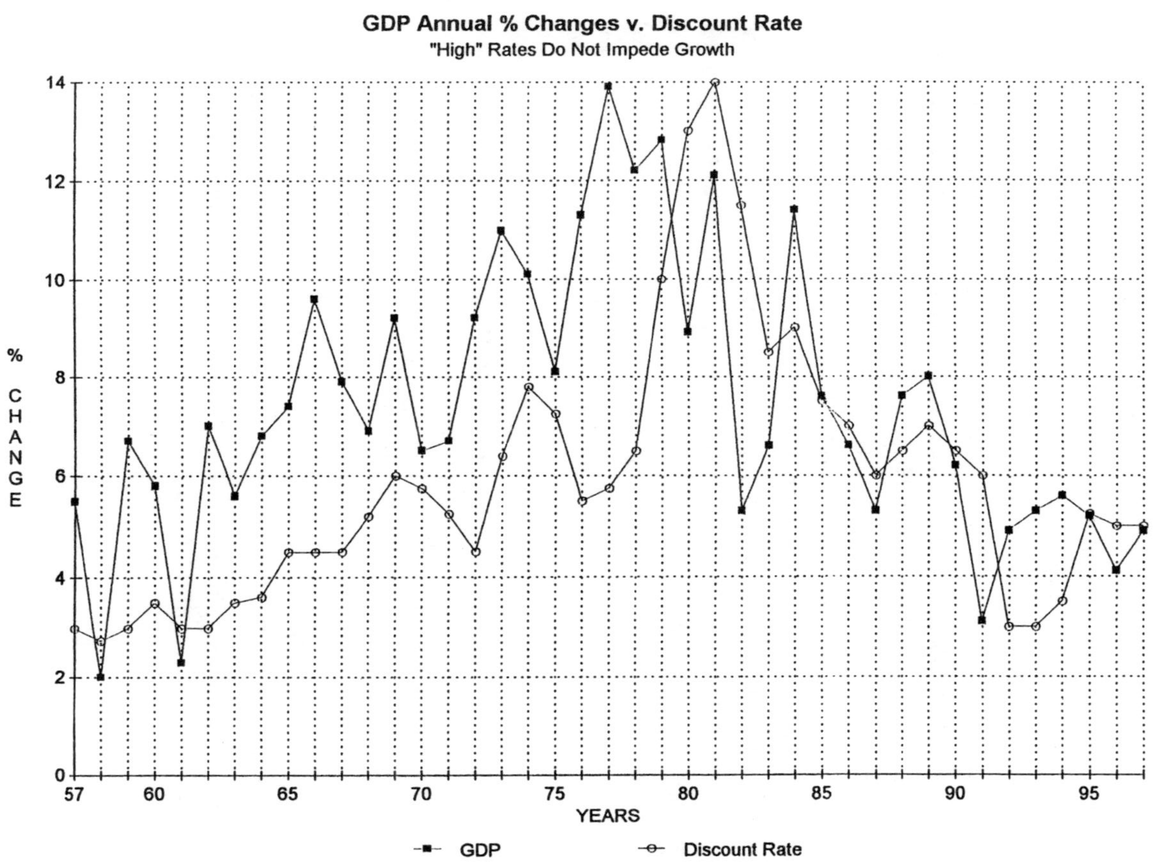

GDP Annual % Changes v. Discount Rate
"High" Rates Do Not Impede Growth
% CHANGE
14
12
10
8
6
4
2
0
57
60
65
70
75
80
85
90
95
YEARS
GDP
Discount Rate

***Argument 2***: If the U.S. "turns on the presses" and prints too much money, w e will have inflation.

***Response:*** The value of any commodity is based on supply and the demand. If we "turn on the presses" the supply will increase. But an increase in supply does not reduce the price if demand increases proportionately. The supply of foreign-made cars and oil is greater than twenty years ago. But the demand has grown greater still. So the price of foreign cars and oil has not fallen.

In a growing economy, the demand for dollars increases to fund the growth. Economic growth in itself, is counter inflationary, because it increases the demand for, and thus the value of, money. This contradicts the Federal Reserve Board, which believes economic growth poses the risk of inflation.

Any decrease in the value of U.S. credit/dollars (inflation) would be both preventable and curable by raising interest rates to increase demand. Federal Reserve Board actions prove this.

Ever since the Reagan years, the government has been "turning on the presses." The value of the dollar has fallen (inflation) at what is considered an acceptable rate by the regulators. Had the Federal Reserve wanted inflation to be even lower, it would have raised interest rates further. There is no necessary relationship between "turning on the presses" and inflation.

***Argument 3***: By competing for investment dollars, the U.S. drains money from other investments, as well as from other nations.

***Response***: Selling U.S. bonds does not drain the world of dollars, nor does it drain money from other investments. Selling debt creates money, which makes more money available for other investments.

The increase in the federal debt by $4 trillion could only be accomplished with a $4 trillion increase in available lending money.

You can't borrow if there are no dollars to lend. And there is no shortage of lending investing funds in America.

Though foreign bonds must compete with U.S. bonds, foreign countries can increase their interest rates to make their debt attractive to lenders. Foreign nations' credit ratings are proportional to the strengths of their economies. When creating money to exchange for U.S. debt, strong nations can offer lower interest rates than can weak nations. A growing U.S. debt does not change this fact.

***Argument 4***: Free Money gives the federal government too much economic power. This "big government" approach is dangerous, leading to totalitarian communism.

***Response:*** True, the greatest danger a nation faces is tyranny from its own government. But this tyranny occurs, not because the central government is too strong, but because the checks and balances are too weak.

Totalitarianism occurs in weak states like the myriad African and island nations. Haiti had one of the weakest central governments imaginable -- and also one of the most tyrannical.

In all dictatorships, is there was no effective countervailing force to the central government. We in the United States own the strongest central government in the world, but we have ample countervailing forces. We have not one, but two houses of Congress, both elected by the people. We have Federal Courts, and a Supreme Court that answer to no politician.

We have an eight-year Presidential term limit. We have individual state governments and state courts, each with great power over regional issues. We have county and local governments and courts that have power over local issues.

We have the Constitution and, perhaps most important, a strong anti-dictatorship history and bias. These checks and balances have made the President of the United States the most powerful man on earth, and also one of the least powerful national leaders. Even with a sympathetic Congress, the President often must struggle to achieve what he wants.

In theory, the more money the federal government is able to spend, the more centralized will be its power and the greater tendency toward socialism (though not communism, which is the absence of government, a never-realized situation.)

But, the system doesn't need to work that way, because the additional money should be distributed by and to those same checks and balances, making them more powerful, too.

It would be difficult to argue that today's federal government is more powerful, oppressive or dictatorial than it was during Franklin Roosevelt's presidency, when the deficit was much smaller. No recent president has had the power to intern thousands of citizens in concentration camps because they were of Japanese heritage -- despite the much greater spending ability by the current government. Social mores exert more leverage than money.

Free Money sits opposite from socialism. Socialism requires "social control" (meaning, "government *control and ownership*") over property and the distribution of money. Socialism is guided by some form of government. In contrast, capitalism with Free Money puts production and the distribution of money into private hands, and is guided by markets.

A purely capitalist society is impossible, since pure capitalism implies no economic power for government -- that is, anarchy. Today, the United States is heavily capitalist, with many socialist elements.

Some may argue that the U.S. is more socialist today than in years past, and the federal debt is higher, proving that a higher debt leads to socialism. I would argue that if the U.S. is more socialist today, it is because the citizens have *wanted* the charitable and protective benefits of socialism, and a higher debt has *allowed* the federal government to abide by the citizens' wishes.

The pendulum swings on such matters, and today you see a move toward reducing certain social benefits such as welfare and other aids to the poor. Sadly, financial reasons are being couched in social arguments.

Having more money to spend enhances a government's ability to control a society, but in a democratic republic, this control comes at the behest of the society itself. The federal government paid for the interstate highway system, but does not control it. The individual states exert far more control.

The federal government funds thousands of projects (sometimes known as "pork") as a way to encourage the development of these projects, yet often retains little, if any, control over these projects.

By creating Free Money, the federal government will provide increased funding for voter-approved projects, with the money, once having entered our economy, directed by capitalist market forces.

*In a perfect execution of "Free Money," the government will create money and distribute most of it to the states, counties and municipalities, for them to spend on local projects.*

Money allocation would be according to population. Each state, county and municipality would receive, for instance, $1 thousand per resident, either to spend as the residents choose or to spend on specific project types.

This localizes the spending, and gives each citizen a greater voice in his country. It also eliminates any danger of a too-strong central government, since the majority of the money would be in the hands of the checks and balances.

We will see that there are no "fair" taxes (Chapter 10). T here is no "fair" method for government allocation of money. A census-based allocation method mitigates concerns about "big government," but it does not take *need* or local costs into consideration. Some states or municipalities need more help than others.

The impoverished town of Harvey, Illinois, with a population of about thirty thousand, and lying twenty miles south of Chicago's Loop, needs massive help in almost every area, from schools to crime control, to infrastructure to health.

The wealthy twin towns of Wilmette and Winnetka, Illinois, with a combined population near forty thousand, and lying twenty miles north of Chicago's Loop, need (and receive) considerably less help from the federal and state governments. Under a purely census-determined allocation, Winnetka/Wilmette would receive more than Harvey. Is this "fair?"

It is preferable to the current system, in which the federal government arbitrarily decides the allocation, a method which could deteriorate into totalitarianism. A census-based allocation is fair *if Harvey, Illinois receives enough to solve its problems.*

*No economy should strive for equality. With Free Money, the economy will strive for sufficiency.*

The old joke is that capitalists want everyone to be equally wealthy, while socialists want everyone to be equally poor. Pure equality implies punishing superior producers while rewarding the inferior producers, a prescription for economic disaster.

***Argument 5:*** We should stay with the established and successful policies. We should change only when an alternative policy has proved to be successful.

***Response:*** There is a myth that debt reduction is an established policy. So-called "established policies" include a witch's brew of government actions, taken under differing circumstances.

There have been policies of deficit and debt increase (Roosevelt and Reagan), deficit decreases with debt increases (most of Clinton's terms), debt maintenance (Truman). Some presidents have had increases and decreases of debt and deficit. Debt decreases were an established policy just prior to the Great Depression.

Not only is it impossible to define "established policy"; it is impossible to define "successful." Were Roosevelt and Reagan successful? Was Carter? Truman? Clinton? Which was most successful?

Finally, Argument #5 asks for proof. How would you prove that each of the following will benefit America: Change the method of taxing, cut Social Security, cut the military, reduce expenditures on welfare, cut education funding, cut infrastructure expenditures, cut medical research? That's what it takes to run a federal surplus.

Some people are taken with the notion that numbers provide reality. Numbers are a quantitative reflection of someone's interpretation. When interpretation is part of the formula, the numbers only represent opinions couched in scientific veneer.

That is why a decision to free money does not rely on numbers, which could be disproved by more numbers. It relies on the logic of the reality around us. Since money is debt, adding debt to the economy adds money to the economy. Since money is wealth, adding money to the economy adds wealth to the economy. No amount of number crunching can disprove that.

***Argument 6:*** In 1998, the government began to run a surplus, yet the economy seems sound.

***Response:*** Total debt in the economy continued to grow; therefore, the total supply of credit/money grew. Further, an economy as large as America's has enormous momentum. It can continue to prosper for months, even after total debt declines.

Using weather as an analogy, the days begin to grow shorter on June 22. Yet the weather continues to warm for another month. Eventually, reduced sunlight takes its toll, and the weather cools.

The same will happen to our economy, and the government will need to produce enormous amounts of money to save us from depression.

When Japan fell into trouble, what was the recommended solution? Cut taxes and increase spending, i.e., Free Money. Although a taste of Free Money has not yet solved all of Japan's problems, it has moved their economy forward. (I say "taste," because a large percent of Japan's debt is owed to Japan's own government, so is not effective debt.)

***Argument 7:*** The psychology is wrong. No matter how good the "Free Money" program is, intuition says not to reduce taxes and increase spending endlessly. Conventional wisdom defeats logic.

***Response:*** In economics, nothing can be proved. Statistics can be produced to support or deny any theory. Accepted theories appeal to our sense of "rightness," to our intuition.

Evolution gave us intuition because it allows us to arrive at decisions quickly. Survival often depends on quick response.

Yet, this powerful shortcut can mislead us. Consider the possibility of constructing four dice, each displaying different numbers. If you roll these dice, die #1 must beat die #2 two-thirds of the time. Die #2 must beat die #3 two-thirds of the time. Die #3 must beat die #4 two-thirds of the time. And, this is the hard one, die #4 must beat die #1 two-thirds of the time.

The implication is that I could hand you all four dice and tell you to select one of them, and no matter which you chose, I could pick another one that would beat you two-thirds of the time. Do you think such dice are possible?

Your intuition tells you such dice are impossible. If #1 beats #2, which beats #3, which in turn beats #4, clearly #1 must beat #4, and by a long margin. But your next thought is, "Why would the author of this book mention these dice if the trick couldn't be done?"

So your intuition changes to tell you there probably are such dice, because you know that as the author, I have the authority to include in this book anything I want. Authority has a profound effect on intuition.

And, in fact, there are such dice, which I will show you on the next page.

| <-Non-Transitive Dice Faces-> | | | | | | |
|---|---|---|---|---|---|---|
| Die #1 | 6 | 6 | 6 | 6 | 6 | 6 |
| Die #2 | 4 | 4 | 4 | 4 | 12 | 12 |
| Die #3 | 10 | 10 | 10 | 3 | 3 | 3 |
| Die #4 | 8 | 8 | 8 | 8 | 1 | 1 |

Explanation: Each die contains six faces. When two dice are rolled, 36 combinations are possible. To win 2/3 of the time, a die must win 24 out of the 36 combinations.

**#1 vs. #2:** Each of the *six* 6's on die #1, will defeat each of the *four* 4's on die #2. Six times four gives a total of 24 wins.
**#2 vs. #3:** Each of the *four* 4's on die #2 defeat each of the *three* 3's on die #3, for a total of twelve wins. Plus, each of the *two* 12's will defeat all *six* of the numbers on die #3. This provides twelve more wins, a total of 24 wins.
**#3 vs. #4:** The *three* 10's on die #3 beat all *six* numbers on die #4. This provides eighteen wins. In addition, each of the *three* 3's defeat each of the *two* 2's, for another six wins. This brings the total to 24 wins.
**#4 vs. #1:** The *four* 8's on die #4 defeat all *six* of the 6's on die #1, for a total of 24 wins.
**Non-intuitive Conclusion:** For every die, there is one other die that will win two-thirds of the time.

The response to psychology or intuition is to change it. The change must be made by authority. One day, an authority (definition: someone with many college degrees and an impressive television manner) will risk his reputation by promoting the "Free Money" concept. He will be attacked.

The concept will be characterized as "something for nothing," ignoring the fact that the world's modern economies are, and *must be*, "something for nothing" (money backed only by "full faith and credit").

Other authorities will speak out and Congress will "neglect" to raise taxes, while it allows spending to increase (as Reagan did). Soon Congress will risk lowering a few taxes (first on the poor, because that is "compassionate," though any tax decrease would equally benefit the poor).

Inflation will be controlled by managing interest rates, thus maintaining demand for credit/dollars. As both the supply and demand for credit/dollars rise, our economy will become healthier, because *a healthy economy is characterized by money growth together with low inflation.*

**Stop and Think:** Sometimes concepts are more easily visualized when they are discussed in their extreme. Imagine two theoretical economies, a "balanced budget" economy and "Free Money": Which economy is more likely to grow? Why? Which economy is more subject to recession and depression? Why?

**In Which of These Economies Would You Prefer to Live?**

1) ***The balanced-budget economy***: Taxation equals spending, so the annual deficit is zero. No new federal money is created. Without money growth, our economy must rely on private debt, which is limited by ability to service debt. When private debt limits are reached, our economy cannot expand.

At that point, the total money supply is fixed. Even the smallest inflation reduces the size of our economy. This is a depression.

The depression decreases tax collection, mandating decreases in spending or increases in tax rates, and leading to ever deeper depressions. Since tax rates cannot exceed 100%, government spending must decline further, and ultimately government spending reaches zero. With no money to spend, the government has no power, which is the definition of anarchy.

The "balanced-budget" economy is a prescription for anarchy.

2) ***Free Money***: Taxes are zero, and borrowing (credit/dollar creation) pays for 100% of U.S. government spending. Raising interest rates allows the U.S. government to borrow and spend more. With this input of money, our economy grows. Sales, profits, employment and salaries increase, because the untaxed public and untaxed business have more disposable income. With higher employment and salaries all forms of investment benefit.

Higher interest rates prevent inflation by balancing the demand for money against the supply. The strong dollar causes our exports to decline and our imports to increase. These imports also help prevent U.S. inflation by allowing foreigners to compete with domestically produced goods.

The economies of the world improve by virtue of their increased exports to the U.S. and their increased earnings of interest dollars. All nations are enriched. As foreign nations have more money, they become more productive.

Science in the "third-world" countries becomes a reality. Instead of being the beggars and welfare recipients of the world, these countries begin to contribute to the world's progress. Free Money succeeds because, money created + inflation controlled + a reward-based economy = economic health.

## *Chapter 10 -- Other Myths, Legends and Leeches*

*"A presidential commission projects that, by 2012, entitlement spending plus interest on the national debt will require all federal tax revenue . . . These trends could plunge America into a swamp of poverty early in the next century." John Attarian,* The World and I, *November 1996*

*"The Fed, (analysts) point out, has a dismal track record when it comes to soft landings – the hoped-for gentle easing of the economy to prevent inflation but maintain a comfortable expansion."* Chicago Tribune, *June 25, 2000.*

### Are Federal Unfunded Mandates Harmful to Our Economy?

Unfunded mandates are government requirements that some entity pay for certain projects or services.

**Stop and Think:** Is an unfunded mandate beneficial, harmful or neutral to our economy as a whole? Why do you feel that way?

There are two kinds of unfunded mandates, federal unfunded mandates and unfunded mandates by all other governmental units. In a federal unfunded mandate, the federal government obligates somebody else to pay for something.

Consider a federal mandate that business pay for environmental cleanups. This requires one business (the "owner") to pay another business (the "cleaner") to clean the environment. One company's outgo is another's income. Money neither is created nor destroyed, so there is no overall economic effect.

If instead, the federal government paid for the cleanups, federal spending would require an increase in government borrowing, which would enrich our economy.

> *Federal unfunded mandates are harmful, because they substitute for federal spending and money creation.*

The federal government never should issue unfunded mandates, because the federal government has an unlimited ability to create the money to pay for anything. It is the sole U.S. entity with this power.

**Are Local Unfunded Mandates Harmful to Our Economy?**

Consider a city mandate that individuals fix the sidewalks in front of their homes. Cities and individuals temporarily create money by borrowing. Because cities have a limited ability to borrow and create money, they are in the same economic position as individuals. Eventually, they must pay the debts back, thereby destroying money.

When the cities tell the citizens they must fix their sidewalks, the citizens must borrow money, which creates money. Eventually, the citizens must pay off the loans, which destroys money. Had the city itself paid for fixing the sidewalks, it too would have borrowed money, and it too eventually would have had to pay off the loan.

The local alternative to an unfunded mandate is a mandate funded through tax dollars. This too, neither creates nor destroys money.

Local unfunded mandates are identical to funded mandates; they neither help nor harm our economy.

**What Is the Absolute Cure for The Social Security and Medicare Messes?**

Predictions are that Social Security will go "bankrupt" within ten or twenty or some other random number of years, depending on the political motives of the prophet. Medicare and Medicaid supposedly either are bankrupt, soon will be bankrupt or are in such dire straights, even the word "bankrupt" is inadequate to describe them.

Before anyone slashes their wrists, let me assure all, *it is impossible for either Social Security or Medicare ever to go bankrupt*, at least not unless a mandated balanced federal budget pushes the entire nation into bankruptcy. This is not a prediction, nor is it a statement related to any estimates of future tax collections or future expenditures.

It is a statement of fact about the financing of these programs. There is no physical or financial or accounting way for them to go bankrupt.

Contrary to popular belief, Social Security and Medicare are not separate entities, whose income and outgo are segregated from the rest of the government. The Social Security taxes you and your employer pay are co-mingled with the federal income taxes you pay. The Social Security "fund" is co-mingled with all the other government money.

Today, because Social Security has an accounting surplus, this "surplus" is used as a partial offset for other government debt, and serves to make the federal debt appear smaller. It's all accounting sleight-of-hand.

Social Security and Medicare can no more go bankrupt or default on their debts than can any other government agency ever go bankrupt or default on its debts. In other words, *never*.

**The Government's Big Pot** The government pays all its debts out of one huge mythical pot. Forget about budgets, appropriations, earmarked funds, balance sheets, etc. These are handy fictions created for political purposes.

To satisfy obligations, all agencies of the government reach into this huge bookkeeping pot and take enough money to pay for things like fighter planes (including the cost overruns that somehow are paid), the overseas junkets taken by Senators, the Congressional perks, and for a rocket here and a park there, a dam, a plane, a road -- and for every other sort of pork-filled, money-driven boondoggle you can imagine -- all from the same, big, mythical pot.

Consider this excerpt from an article in the April 12, 1997 Chicago Tribune:

> *Some speculate that the (federal highway trust) fund will grow to $50 billion or more by 2002 . . . So ample is the fund . . . that 4.3 cents a gallon . . . are diverted to help eradicate the deficit . . . There is congressional support for returning most of the 4.3 cents to the highway trust fund . . . But (Ralph DiGennaro, director of Taxpayers for Common Sense said) "To take this money away from deficit reduction and use it to spend more money is outrageous . . ."*

Do you believe, as these folks seem to, there is a separate tub of dollars locked away in Washington, D.C., with a label on it reading, "Federal Highway Trust?" Do you believe someone scoops out 4.3% of these dollars to cut the deficit?

Mr. DiGennaro and Congress are referring to internal bookkeeping entries, easily and often manipulated. There is no money in anything called the "Federal Highway Trust."

All money is credit, and only creditors own money. So, the federal government has little money, because it seldom is a creditor (except when it lends to nations, students, small businesses, etc.)

The next dollar the federal government spends on roads will be borrowed, just as all other government expenditures are. The government has no spare money to be used for paying down the debt. Mr. DiGennaro should walk into the Treasury and ask to see where even one dollar's worth of the Federal Highway Trust fund is stored.

To own money, the Federal Highway Trust would have to become a creditor. But who would be the debtor? No one owes the Federal Highway Trust anything, except perhaps the Treasury, and internal debts don't count as money. (Otherwise, you could make yourself rich by declaring that your left pocket is a creditor to your right pocket.)

Social Security and Medicare too, are paid out of that big pot. And the government never runs short. Have you ever heard of a U.S. government check bouncing? You never will.

Why? Because once that check is written, budgets, appropriations, etc. lose all meaning. The check comes out of the pot, and the pot is bottomless.

The theoretical bottom of the pot is the fiction known as the "debt ceiling." But the debt ceiling is raised any time we get near it. If it didn't, the world's economies would go into free-fall.

Remember the recent game of "chicken" between the Democrats and the Republicans regarding the debt ceiling. When Congress failed to raise the ceiling, President Clinton had all "nonessential" workers stay home. In other words, he began to *allocate* government funds to those uses that were most politically necessary.

*This allocation of funds disproves the theory that one agency of government can go bankrupt while the government survives.* Social Security and Medicare could go bankrupt only if the government wanted them to.

The government can pay for Medicare and Social Security by raising the debt ceiling, which allows more money to be produced. However, Congress is working hard to find ways to remove the government from any such obligations, and to make Social Security and Medicare taxpayer funded, break-even programs.

If Congress succeeds, our economy will suffer. Not only would our economy lose the benefit of money creation, but it is unlikely that Social Security or Medicare can be self-funded and still provide the services an aging population will need.

Recent years have produced much talk about privatizing Social Security. The concept seems to be that the investment markets offer a higher return than do government bonds, which erroneously are believed to be Social Security's current source of investment income.

The first fallacy: Any so-called "income" Social Security receives from investments in government securities, merely represents an accounting transfer of funds from one government account to another, not true income. (The right hand calls it "income"; the left hand calls it "outgo," and nothing has happened.)

The second fallacy: "Privatizing" represents the transfer of income from low risk (government) investments, to higher risk (all other) investments. How increasing the investment risk will solve Social Security's problems, is a question no one can answer.

When we have a recession, and the securities markets fall, a privatized Social Security would be unable to meet its commitments, which would worsen the economy. The downward spiral would lead to economic failure.

Even without the threat of a recession, privatizing is nonsense. Assume Social Security is invested in stocks and the stock market rises. To pay recipients, Social Security would have to sell stocks (Can you visualize the problems with the federal government trading in the stock market?) The buyers of those stocks would send their money to Social Security, which then would transfer it to recipients.

What has happened? In effect, Social Security recipients have been given stock by the federal government, stock which was purchased by Social Security taxes. No new money was created. That is the situation we have now. The economy sends money to Social Security recipients, with the government acting as the transfer agent. Privatizing solves nothing.

We even have heard of a scheme in which privatized accounts would be required to invest in government securities, for safety. This, of course, would result in no change from the current system, except another bureaucracy (to monitor the transfers) would be created. Taxpayers would continue to pay for everything, directly for investment principal and indirectly (through taxes) for investment income.

It would amount to the same transfer we now have, money flowing from some citizens to other citizens, with no money created.

All efforts to reduce the government's role in the funding of Social Security and Medicare will result in economic disaster for the sick, the elderly and for our economy as a whole.

The solution, which should be obvious at this stage of this book: Eliminate all Social Security and Medicare taxes, and have both programs *totally* funded through money creation (federal government borrowing). Raise the Social Security payments to a level that will allow people to live on them. And end the tax on Social Security payments. Why send it to the people if you're going to take it back?

Pay enough for Medicare to eliminate the sad, frightening circumstances of people being denied adequate medical services because they cost too much. (People who should have "CAT" scans don't receive them because they are too expensive. New mothers are being tossed out of the hospital after one day. Hospitals are understaffed and hospital staff is overworked.)

There is no economic reason why the federal government cannot pay for all the medical care we need, either by direct payments, or by payments funneled through the states and other local governments.

Don't worry about whether the doctors and hospitals will get rich. These are *our* doctors and *our* hospitals, and they employ *our* people and they spend money in *our* economy. If we make the doctors and hospitals rich, there will be more doctors and hospitals and better health care and more money for all of us.

Increased government spending on Medicare and on Social Security would make our economy wealthy and our citizens healthy -- and vice versa.

**Which Types of Taxes Are Most Harmful to the U.S. Economy?**

Local governments do not have an unlimited ability to create money. When a local government runs up against its debt limit, it has no option other than to tax.

So long as the municipality remains at its debt limit, the destruction of money (taxing) equals the creation of money (borrowing), and there is no net adverse effect on the U.S. economy. (The local economy may be harmed however, if business and consumers move to a more tax-favorable site.)

If the local government uses taxes to move below its debt limit, more money will be destroyed than created. This harms the U.S. economy.

All federal taxes hurt the U.S. economy, because all federal taxes reduce either the actual or potential amount of money in our economy.

The answer to the headlined question is:

1. All federal taxes are harmful
2. All local taxes by governments not at their debt limit are harmful. Taxes by local governments at their debt limit are neutral.

## Which Taxes Are the Most and the Least Fair?

> **Stop and Think:** Although taxes hurt our economy, the reality is, taxes will not disappear tomorrow. Have you any thoughts about the types of taxes that are fairest? Is this a worthwhile economic discussion?

The American ethic is based on "getting ahead" and on "fairness." However, being ahead seems unfair to those who are behind. Taxes can be levied in a variety of ways, all justifiable as "fair" and condemned as "unfair."

***A unit tax on individuals***: Each person pays the same tax (similar to an airport departure tax). This tax is fair, because it treats every individual equally. This tax is unfair, because it takes as much from the poor as from the rich.

***Sin taxes*** on cigarettes, liquor, entertainment, gambling, restaurants, etc. are fair, because they tax things we do not need. These taxes are unfair, because they arbitrarily designate certain items as not being needed. (Is an apple "needed?")

***Sales taxes*** are fair, because each person pays according to his consumption. Sales taxes are unfair, because they place a burden on low income people, who spend a greater percentage of their income and save/invest less.

***Flat-rate income tax*** is fair, because each person pays the same rate. These taxes are unfair, because the poor cannot afford to pay as high a rate as the wealthy.

***Progressive rate income tax*** is fair, because high earners can afford to pay a higher rate. This tax is unfair, because even at a flat rate, higher earners would pay more. A progressive rate compounds the unfairness.

***Tax on Social Security benefits*** is fair, because social security is just another form of income. These taxes are unfair, because income tax already was paid on Social Security deposits. It is a double tax.

***Inheritance tax*** is fair, because wealthy families can afford to pay more. This tax is unfair, because taxes already have been paid on the assets being inherited. It is a double tax.

***Personal property tax*** is fair, again because the wealthy can afford to pay more. This tax is unfair, because taxes already have been paid on the earnings needed to acquire the assets. It is another double tax.

***Tax on stock dividends*** is fair, because dividends are no different from any other income. This tax is unfair, because companies cannot deduct the cost and already have paid taxes on the earnings. It is one more double tax.

***Taxes on corporations*** are fair because business should pay its share. These taxes are unfair, because they penalize workers by reducing corporations' ability to hire and to pay salaries and benefits.

All taxes are fair and unfair, depending on whose toes are pinched. Discussions of tax fairness are sophistry, demagoguery or both. The question of tax fairness is not an appropriate subject for economics' discussions. Perhaps it is more appropriate for a psychology seminar.

The real question should be: Is that tax helpful or harmful to the overall economy? In nearly all cases, the tax will be harmful. (Exceptions may be taxes collected to curtail harmful items that cannot be eliminated by law. These include taxes on guns, drugs, cigarettes, etc.)

**Which Taxes Should be Cut First?**

When Congress, the President and the American people accept the "Free Money" concept, federal taxes will not suddenly disappear. Most people believe gradualism is prudent.

Which taxes should be cut first? All taxes are unfair. And, over time, all tax cuts help the economy equally. The question then revolves around two issues: Which tax cuts are most politically acceptable? And, which tax cuts would help boost the economy fastest?

I believe the answer to both issues is the same. Eliminate Social Security and Medicare taxes. These two taxes effectively are regressive, placing a much greater proportionate burden on low earners than on high earners.

The person earning less than $30 thousand annually, may pay more for FICA than for income tax. The person earning $300 thousand, spends only a minuscule fraction of his earnings on FICA.

Further, business pays half of FICA, so the entire business constituency would favor these cuts.

Cutting taxes on the poor and on business is politically acceptable. It also would have immediate benefits to the economy. FICA is collected early in the year, sooner on average than income taxes payments, which are spread through the year.

Money works its way through the economy, and ultimately benefits everyone. But the most immediate benefits, both real and perceived, would be to the poor and to business.

*Thus, "Free Money" could be referred to as the "trickle-up" theory*

## Is the U.S. Trade Deficit Too High and Should It Be Reversed Into a Surplus?

In 1991 the official U.S. trade deficit was about $50 billion. In 2000, the deficit was more than $350 billion, having increased during the economic boom years.

> **Stop and Think:** If we raise interest rates to prevent inflation, we strengthen U.S. money, which reduces exports, increases imports and so, increases the “trade deficit.” Is an increased trade deficit harmful or helpful to our economy?

Experts believe money is scarcer, more valuable or harder to produce than the goods and services it buys. How else can you explain the concerns about the “trade deficit?”

**All Buying and Selling Is Barter**

The trade deficit is the difference between the dollars we export versus the dollar cost of the goods and services we export. Conventional wisdom says it is healthier for our economy to import more credit/dollars and to export more goods and services.

What a strange thought. Money is neither more valuable nor less valuable than what it is exchanged for.

> *Money has exactly the same value as the goods and services it buys*

If this weren't true, no one would trade goods and services for money.

Any exchange of money for goods or services can be considered a barter transaction. One person has money; the other has goods or services. The person with money values the other person's goods or services as high as or higher than the value of the money. The other person has the opposite feelings. So they decide to make an exchange.

Who is better off after the exchange? Clearly, neither. Yet experts criticize our sending too much of this easily replaced commodity called "money" across the ocean, when all we receive is supposedly less valuable (yet harder to replace) goods and services.

Imagine you are on a boat that has a money-printing machine aboard. You can print all the money you wish, but you're short of food.

Along comes another boat, the passengers of which want to trade their food for some of your money. Would you resist? We live on such a boat. It's called "America."

The so-called "trade deficit" should be called a trade *surplus,* because we receive more goods than we ship out. We export the most easily created of any commodity on earth (money), a commodity that has no intrinsic value, and one which we can produce merely by turning on the printing presses. We receive goods with intrinsic value and which are far more difficult to create.

In summary:

> 1) Every export is another country's import. The world's net balance of trade always equals zero. When the U.S. trade balance is positive (more money received), some other nation's trade balance is negative.
>
> According to conventional wisdom, all nations' economies cannot be enriched simultaneously. Half the world always suffers a trade "deficit."

2) The U.S. can offset its money loss by creating more money – something weaker countries are less able to do. The U.S. never will run out of money, because we have the capability to produce an unlimited amount.

Using Free Money, the U.S. will have a positive outflow of money (trade deficit), while creating more money. This will strengthen the economies of other countries. These countries then will become better trading partners, and their imports will strengthen U.S. industry.

**What Are the "Free Money" Truths Concerning the "Universal" Beliefs?**

Now we can discuss the "universal beliefs" expressed in Chapter 1:

1. *The U.S. federal debt is too high: It burdens taxpayers.* False. A growing economy needs more money. The federal debt is largely owed to American citizens (the creditors) and represents money in the pockets of future generations.

   But even were all the debt owed to foreigners, debt cannot be a "burden" to creditors. It only can be a burden to a debtor. The federal debt never is a burden to our debtor government, since the government has no difficulty producing the money to pay it. The only economic burden taxpayers face is taxes, which have no economic benefit.
2. *A growing federal debt is inflationary.* False. The value of money depends on supply and demand. A growing debt does increase supply. However, when the Federal Reserve increases interest rates, the demand for money increases and inflation stops. The proof: Despite a fast growing federal debt in recent years, inflation has remained low. Whenever it starts

to rise, the Federal Reserve raises interest rates and stops inflation in its tracks.

3. *The savings rate in America is too low.* Partly false. It depends on what kind of saving. To save by investing in stocks, real estate, stock mutual funds, precious metals, collectibles, etc. adds no money to our economy. The Great Depression proved this, when people "saved" by purchasing stocks. To save by lending (opening bank accounts, buying bonds, CD's, annuities and other financial paper) does help our economy by creating credit/dollars.
4. *Americans today have too much personal debt.* False. Private debt adds money to our economy. Though bankruptcies have increased lately, that is due more to the liberalization of bankruptcy laws, rather than to economics. Despite rising debt and bankruptcies, our economy has continued to grow. The evidence is that high private debt has had no negative effect on our economy as a whole, though it can be a problem for any individual.
5. *A growing federal debt forces interest rates up.* False. An increase in government borrowing does not require offering high interest rates. Since borrowing creates money, an increase in borrowing creates an increase in funds available for further borrowing.
6. *Low interest rates make borrowing easier, which helps the U.S. economy grow.* False. Low interest rates make *borrowing* more attractive, but *lending* less attractive. The U.S. government's borrowing to pay interest on its notes benefits our economy. Interest rates have had no long-term effect on our economy, despite the negative illusion created by short-term changes in stock, bond and real estate markets.

7. *The U.S. trade deficit is too high and should be reversed into a surplus*. False. The higher the trade deficit, the more the world's economies are enriched. "Trade deficit" means the U.S. receives more goods and services from overseas than it sends away -- a "goods and services surplus." Sending money overseas is no loss to the U.S. which can and does create all the money it needs, but it does benefit other countries by adding to their wealth.
8. *Taxes are necessary to pay for federal spending*. False. Money (federal debt) pays for federal spending. Taxes destroy money by destroying federal credit.
9. *Business should pay its "fair share" of federal taxes*. False. Tax "fairness" is meaningless. All taxes hurt our economy and the poor. Business taxes are the most immediately harmful, because they directly impede business.
10. *There is no affordable solution to rising crime, health care and Social Security costs, poverty, military needs, a declining ecosystem and a deteriorating infrastructure*. False. The affordable solution to all these needs is greater federal funding. The federal government should pay for more police, more doctors, nurses, hospitals and research, antipollution and conservation measures and for better transportation and communication facilities.

## *Chapter 11 -- How Have Words Deceived Us?*

*"The last time governments were this clueless about a worldwide financial crisis was the 1930s. And it's useful to remember that the policy wonks really botched things back then, turning a serious recession into the decade long Great Depression by doing exactly the wrong things: withholding liquidity from banks and markets when they should have opened the taps, raising tariffs when they should have lowered them and zealously trying to balance their budgets when they should have been spending their way out of the abyss."* Newsweek Magazine, *December 8, 1997*

**Stop and Think:** Most people are wrong regarding the ten beliefs discussed in the previous chapter. Despite overwhelming evidence to the contrary, the beliefs persist. Why do you think that is?

The primary reasons for the misunderstandings have to do with semantics and tradition. An English teacher once told me, "There are no synonyms." She meant it was rare for any two words to have the same interpretation. There are slight differences, even between very similar words, and these differences tend to change and blend through time.

You may use an accurate word to describe a situation, but the word may be so charged with other meanings as to convey an inaccurate interpretation of the situation.

> I am prudent; you are cautious; he is fearful; they are cowardly. I am ingenious; you are clever; he is crafty; they are sneaky.

Tradition gives to words, special meanings, not explicit in the words themselves. Consider the word "deficit," which is related to "deficient." These words indicate something has less than something else, but deliver negative connotations, and are used in a pejorative manner.

When you talk about a diet, you say it is "low" or "light" or "free" of calories. However, when you discuss the starvation diet in African countries, you these diets are deficient in calories.

When you talk about a food that is low in calcium, you may say it is "deficient" in calcium. But a food never is "deficient" in lead or arsenic, though it may be low in these substances, too. "Deficit" and its cousins, are words with negative connotations.

"Debt" is a bad word. Consider which is worse: "He is in *debt* to the bank for a million dollars," vs. "He has a line of *credit* for a million dollars." Going into debt seems much worse than using credit, though both are identical.

"Saving" is good for America, though saving requires investing in bank accounts and Treasury securities, which are debt. It always was considered patriotic to buy U.S. Savings bonds, though this increases the national debt, which conventional wisdom considers bad for the country.

Compare, "I have saved for my son's education by purchasing a $10 thousand Treasury bond," vs. "I have just helped push the government $10 thousand further into debt."

When you "deposit" money in your bank savings account, you help your bank boast about the size of its "deposits," which in fact, are debts.

When you lend money to the federal government, you deposit money with the government. U.S. government *deposits* exceed $five trillion. Doesn't that sound better than saying the government *owes* $five trillion? Yet the two statements mean the same.

The traditional connotations of such words as "deficit," "debt" and "saving" have confused the beliefs about our economy. The traditional accounting terms used in corporate reports (debt, deficit, spend, budget, equity, balance), and in personal experience (save, waste, cost, owe, burden) do not describe a nation's money systems. They mislead.

**A Glossary for "Free Money"**

Using different words can better describe the U.S. economy:

| ***Common Term*** | ***True Meaning*** |
|---|---|
| credit (debt) | money or deposits |
| federal debt | economic surplus or money or federal deposits |
| federal deficit | Money or economic surplus |
| federal surplus | Economic deficit |
| trade deficit | import surplus |
| lend | create money |
| spend (government) | send money to the economy |
| reduce debt | destroy money |
| to tax | to confiscate and destroy money |
| a tax | a money confiscation/destruction system |
| owes | has created (money) |
| save (government) | avoid distributing (money) |
| waste (noun) | less productive money distribution |
| budget | money distribution goal or limit |
| our economy | business |

Here are two sample paragraphs. The first uses the common, misleading terms. The second, with the same intended meaning, uses "Free Money" terms.

1) ***Common, misleading language regarding the U.S. economy:***

The U.S. federal debt has grown to $5 trillion, which amounts to about $20 thousand owed by each person in America. As federal spending rises and voters resist taxes, the U.S. must borrow more, so the deficit increases.

The experts want higher taxes to pay off this debt, because they believe debt is a financial burden on our economy and on future generations. Many people even wish the government would run a surplus.

The Democrats, long branded the "tax and spend" party, wish to reduce government borrowing by increasing taxes.

The Republicans, who also believe our economy has too much debt, propose a similar plan, which emphasizes reduced taxes and reduced spending.

Very few people understand that our economy would benefit by increasing the deficit, increasing spending, reducing taxes and increasing the national debt.

2) ***Free Money terms:***

The economic surplus (or, deposits with the U.S. government) has grown to more than $5 trillion, which amounts to about $20 thousand owned by each person in America. As federal money distribution increases and voters resist the confiscation of their dollars, the U.S. must create more money.

The experts want the government to confiscate money and destroy it, because they believe owning money puts a financial burden on business and on future generations. Many people even wish the government would take more money from the economy than it puts in.

The Democrats, long branded as the "confiscate money, distribute money" party, wish to confiscate even more money.

The Republicans, who also believe business has too much money, propose a similar plan, which emphasizes less money confiscation and less money distribution.

Very few people understand that business would benefit by increasing the growth and distribution of money, reducing the confiscation of money and putting more money in the hands of the people.

**The Voice Brought in From the Wilderness**

The world's governments rely on conventional wisdom about their economies (Deficits are bad; taxes are prudent, etc.). They lurch from one economic crisis to another.

Economics refuses to believe its own research. The dramatically increased U.S. debt provided a test of the "deficit-hurts-the-economy" theory. The test proved there is no relationship between federal debt and a negative economic outcome. In fact, the contrary is true. Economists ignore the results.

We Americans want many things. We want a strong Social Security system, one we can rely on to protect us when we retire. We want Medicare and Medicaid systems that will help us when we're poor or old, throughout our lives, no matter what our age or financial condition. We want street crime to disappear.

We want major improvements in the education we give our children. We want to modernize our infrastructure. We want profitable investments. We want our ecology to be protected. We want a strong military. We want low inflation. And we want lower taxes.

We want many things, but what do the experts say? We can't have both lower taxes and more spending on social issues. We can't have low inflation, while we cut taxes and spend more. We can't afford Social Security and Medicare, even in their present form, let alone improved versions.

The experts say we spend too much and we save too little, and in the story of the ant and the grasshopper, we are the wastrel grasshoppers. To lead good lives, we must suffer.

They are wrong. Free Money allows us to have it all, and we don't need to suffer.

The academics are wrong, partly because their gene pool is too small. This generation's economists learned from last generation's. And they, in turn, learned from the previous generation's. This incestuous coupling of the misinformed, allows misinformation to pass unimpeded through the generations.

They watched the federal debt rise 500% in sixteen years. They attended the longest period of sustained growth and prosperity in our history. They lived through a wonderful period of low inflation and wealth accumulation. They witnessed almost every commonly held economic theory being dashed on the rocks of reality. Yet, as Sherlock Holmes said, "They see but they do not observe."

Years ago I saw a very funny movie containing a scene in which a woman caught her husband in bed with another woman. The naked husband sits up and says, "Are you going to believe me or your eyes?" The experts want us to believe them, not our eyes.

There is an America where Social Security, Medicare and Medicaid are healthy, where education and infrastructure are superior. There is an America where a strong military, a powerful economy and ample social benefits coexist with low inflation.

That America enjoys the benefits of Free Money. It stands within our reach, asking to be embraced. It is ours for the taking.

We beg those in power to discard the clichés of conventional wisdom and to create a fresh, workable "Free Money" America that will deliver us to a healthy, educated, efficient, safe and secure world.

You, the reader, can begin the battle with a letter to your Congressional representatives. Ask them to abandon platitudes. Make them think. It is what you pay them to do. It is time to free money.

## *Chapter 12 – The End of Federal Borrowing*

The most important question in all of economics is, "A growing economy must have a growing supply of money. ***Where will we find the money to grow our economy***?"

And as we have seen, the answer is, the federal government continually must add money to the economy. The government does this by spending more than it taxes. It creates a "deficit," the amount of federal "debt" added each year.

We already have proposed that federal taxes be eliminated, as an unnecessary, damaging relic from times past, when money was backed by scarce commodities. There is a group of economists known as chartalists, who hold that taxes have another function: giving value to money.

Their philosophy is: People are required to use money to pay taxes. Without taxes, money – specifically federal money – would not be in demand. People eventually would drift to other forms of payment – gold, silver, grain and such.

While we do not agree with the proposition, we also do not propose the elimination of *all* taxes, only federal taxes. There would remain billions of dollars in state and local taxes, enough to satisfy the most ardent chartalist.

A growing supply of money is necessary for a growing economy, and federal debt is a form of money. Because T-bills, T-notes and T-bonds are federal debt and a form of money, we have proposed that the federal debt be greatly expanded – more T-bills, T-notes and T-bonds.

*Now we propose that, not only federal taxes but federal debt, be eliminated.*

> **Stop and Think:** What would happen if the federal government neither taxed nor borrowed? Where would it obtain the money to pay for goods and services?

We have shown that the federal government has the unlimited ability to produce money by borrowing. Does it have the unlimited ability to produce money without borrowing?

Visualize this: The federal government creates a checking account called "Money Created." In the same way Congress creates the debt ceiling, Congress arbitrarily could determine the credit balance of the Money Created checking account.

When the federal government wishes to spend money on goods and services, it issues a check or electronic transfer from this account. The recipient of the check deposits it in a bank, and the bank is credited for the amount of the check – exactly as happens now.

With each check or electronic transfer issued, the amount of money in the economy grows, and the economy prospers.

Why eliminate federal borrowing? Federal borrowing gives the false impression that the government is "in debt." Those frightening words, as misleading as they may be, have caused endless mischief. When borrowing is ended, the whole concept of federal debt, potential bankruptcy and fiscal imprudence disappears, and the government can take positive steps to grow our economy and improve our society.

But isn't federal debt a tool against inflation? The Fed raises interest rates to cure or prevent inflation, and these rates are reflected in what federal securities pay.

The Fed adjusts interest rates paid by banks, and these rates are reflected in *all* debt, personal corporate and state and local governmental. Even without federal debt, there is plenty of debt for the Fed to manipulate in its fight against inflation and deflation.

Because federal debt is unnecessary and harmful, the creation, sale, purchase and servicing of federal debt is a waste of economic resources. The thousands of people occupied with this useless activity could benefit the economy in more productive pursuits.

Gone would be the fears that foreign nations might grow "tired" of buying our debt. Gone would be the concerns about our children having to "pay" the debt. Gone would be the misleading "debt clocks" one sees on the Internet.

The government would return to its primary function: creating money to support the economy and to improve our lives.

## Chapter 13 -- The Three-Step Formula for Prosperity

In summary, I recommend this three-step formula for prosperity:

1) ***Eliminate federal taxes***. Sending money to the government is "sending coals to Newcastle." The government is a producer of money. When you send your money to the government, the government simply destroys it.

First to disappear: All Social Security and Medicare taxes. This will be politically popular, as these regressive taxes impact businesses, and low-to-middle income people most. The politician who ends FICA will be a hero.

The federal government will create the money to support retirement and health care.

2) ***Eliminate federal borrowing***. As a producer of money, a sovereign government never needs to borrow money. This is an inefficient, actually harmful, exercise that provides no economic benefit. Federal borrowing provides the semantic impression the government is "in debt," a concept people find repugnant.

No borrowing; no debt; no wrong-headed hand-wringing about we citizens owing the debt.

3) ***Establish a national, money-supply goal***. Include in it all the things currently called "debt." The government will create a checking account called "Money Created." It will add money to this account whenever needed. It will write checks and make transfers from the Money Created account to pay for all goods and services.

That will be the system for federal money creation in our economy. Congress will determine how much money should be added to the Money Created account, thus giving Congress control over money creation. The Fed will continue to control interest rates and inflation.

Congress will spend what it deems necessary on retirement, health care, the military, the infrastructure, education, crime prevention and other national needs.

We will have freed ourselves from the tyranny of semantics and the irrational fear of federal debt. We will prosper as no nation has before us.

-END-

## *Appendix -- E-Mail On the Concord Coalition List and Other Correspondence*

*"I'm proud of a society that allocates its resources so people can live a decent quality of life. But the costs (of dialysis) are escalating, so we have to come up with some scheme of allocation." David Thomas, director of the medical humanities program at Loyola University Medical Center, Maywood, IL. (Chicago Tribune, March 1, 1998.)*

*"Should a 60-year-old guy in a nursing home, who is demented, receive dollars for dialysis versus a 100-year-old guy who's writing poetry, or someone like [author] James Michener?" Dr. David Albala, associate professor of urology at Loyola University Medical Center, Maywood, IL. (Chicago Tribune, March 1, 1998.)*

The Concord Coalition, a group headquartered in Marist College, is a strong advocate for balancing the federal budget and even running a federal surplus. Concord's leaders say the federal government should even become a net lender.

Members of Congress helped found this group.

I joined their E-mail discussion list, because it opposed everything *Free Money* stands for. The purpose was to check my theories against the most antagonistic group -- sincere, intelligent people, who have given thought to the problem, and who disagree with me.

Here is a sampling of the hundreds of E-mail messages, sent and received. You'll see the views opposing Free Money. Perhaps you still hold some of these views. If so, you'll have a chance to see your ideas expressed, and my comments.

The letters have been edited -- I hope fairly -- for space. I have disguised the names of my fellow list members. I am, of course, "RMM."

October 19, 1997

C: [Re. his statistics disagreeing with the "Free Money" concept.] There are methods for establishing validity which are quantitative and are in between intuitive rhetoric and rigorous proof.

RMM: "Between intuitive rhetoric and rigorous proof" is pure intuitive, since one small variable in a formula can change the results.

Experts have massive statistics available to them, yet are puzzled about the lack of inflation. Top economists – PhDs -- thought the scarcity of labor forces inflation. They have been proved wrong.

Low unemployment is not a necessary cause for inflation. Neither is high debt. So long as inflation is prevented through interest rate control, we could have 0% unemployment and ten times the debt, and no inflation..

October 19, 1997

W: Quantitative data exists, which refute some of your ideas about the advisability of the U.S. to support ever-increasing Federal debt.

RMM: The analyses to which you refer, showed federal debt changes did not always parallel GDP changes. I agree, and have said it myself. *Total* Debt growth is necessary for GDP growth, and federal debt is but one component of Total Debt.

October 20, 1997

R: Challenge to Rodger: Take an open poll and see if you can get a majority of the people on this list to agree with your "all money is debt/all debt is money" assertion.

RMM: I don't believe all debt is money. All *financial* debt is money. There are forms of debt that are not money. If you owe me a bushel of wheat, that's not money. If you owe me $1,000, that is money.

Please tell the group to name one form of money in America that is not debt.

October 20, 1997

B: Debt is a condition of owing. I have $23 in my wallet. I am not in debt to anyone for that $23 . . . I have money in savings and a number of other investments for the kid's college and our retirement. These amounts do not put me in the red. I owe the accumulated amounts to no one (as I would if they were debt). To the question, Is all money debt? NO.

RMM: The owner of debt is called a "creditor." As the creditor, you do not owe. The debtor owes. As for the money you have in savings, the bank is the debtor. It owes you the money you lent to it (deposited).

As for the $23 in green printed paper, the federal government is the debtor. It owes you what gives the $23 its value, namely "full faith and credit."

October 22, 1997

M: The gold in Fort Knox offers implicit support for the dollar. That would dispel your argument that all money is debt, since the full faith and credit is supported by a substance which is not debt.

RMM: If gold really did back our dollar (which it doesn't), money still would be debt. The government would owe gold to the bearer of a dollar. To owe is to be in debt.

However, gold is a minor asset in our economy. It does no more to support our full faith and credit than does any other asset. Some people feel gold has a special security, beyond what aluminum, steel, oil reserves, real estate, Mount Rushmore, the great lakes or any other U.S. assets offer. It doesn't. It's just a commodity, whose price is based on supply and demand, and has no relationship to money. Our money is not backed by gold, in Fort Knox or elsewhere.

October 23, 1997

D: I would consider a $5 loan to a friend to be financial debt, but I certainly wouldn't consider it money.

RMM: Do you agree that a note for $500 million constitutes money? If so, do you believe that the amount of the loan decides the difference between money and non-money?

Do you agree that a $5 debt to a bank is money. What is your dividing line between money and non-money? The $500 million note, the $5 debt to the bank and the $5 debt to your friend all are money, though their liquidity and current market value differ.

D: I would be curious as to whether this assertion and the five conclusions you draw from it have been expressed by others in the public arena and, if so, where? I am willing to look at anybody's arguments but am willing to spend more time looking at those that have survived some degree of public scrutiny.

RMM: Many other people oppose the notion of a balanced federal budget. If that were not true, there would be no need for a Concord Coalition. Even Concord has stated that if we entered a recession or depression, deficit spending would be necessary to cure it.

October 24, 1997

W: I own a bank. High interest rates inhibit refinancings and new purchases of capital goods: notably, cars and homes.

RMM: In the very short term, a few months at best. Very few people, who want a home or a car, would decide never to buy until rates come down. Typically they wait a bit, but if rates stay up, they'll adjust to the new rates. I bought my first house with a 5% mortgage. Today mortgages are around 8% and houses are selling as fast as ever.

W: Businesses will borrow less if the economy is weakened by low consumer demand.

RMM: True in the very short term, but business will not decide against borrowing, just because rates are high. Interest is one of the lowest costs most businesses encounter. While a business that wants to build a plant or buy a machine may delay a short time, if the need remains, it will borrow..

W: Mr. Mitchell, please supply us with your time-series so I can put it in my econometrics model and I will confirm or deny your proposition (that high interest rates don't hurt business).

[Interest rate and GDP data given for the years 1957 through 1996]

RMM: Since the GDP almost always rises from year to year, your theory would be that high interest rates should cause the GDP to rise less, and low interest rates should cause the GDP to rise more. Correct?

Not only is there no correlation between high interest rates and low GDP growth, but surprisingly, there is somewhat of a reverse correlation. It may relate to the extra interest the government pays to the economy.

October 25, 1997

K: The government is not some ethereal, virtual-reality construct. It's you, me and every other American taxpayer.

RMM: You are not the government and the government is not you. You pay taxes. The government receives taxes. You can go bankrupt. The government cannot.

K: John Q. Investor (or foreign investors) will be repaid with funds taken from the wages of taxpayers without regard to the benefits they may derive from the indebtedness.

RMM: That's the problem with taxation. It never can be fair. It always hurts the poor. And it never can be beneficial. It destroys money. Instead of eliminating the benefit (money), why not eliminate the problem (taxes)?

K: No taxes. Unlimited money to satisfy unlimited human desires. No worries about ever repaying indebtedness . . . just print more money. It seems we're back to the free lunch theory.

RMM: The government takes a worthless piece of paper, prints it green and declares it is worth $1, $5, $10, etc. There is no backing for this piece of paper except full faith and credit. The government creates money out of nothing. Money is a free lunch.

K: Do you honestly believe that any legitimate government can function and retain a credit worthy status, while operating under a tax-free system whose stated purpose is to print enough money so that every member of its population may have their every want and desire satisfied?

RMM: The federal government has printed trillions of paper dollars, backed by nothing and accepted by everyone. Why do we accept those paper dollars? We can't redeem them for anything except more dollars.

The federal debt exceeds $5 trillion, so clearly taxes are not supporting the debt. We've already mentioned a great deal of evidence that taxes are harmful, especially to poor people. Why do we want to continue a harmful practice if there is no evidence it's necessary?

K: Although every one of us would dearly love to see it, one doesn't have to reference the Weirmar Republic, Brazil or Mexico to blow such wishful thinking out of the water.

RMM: Merely reciting a list of history's economic failures proves nothing. But regarding Germany – how could that destitute country, whose money became so worthless, people carried it in wheelbarrows, build a huge and powerful war machine?

How did they pay millions of soldiers, and build planes, tanks and guns, etc.? Answer: They printed the money to do it. Those soldiers and industrialists didn't work for nothing.

K: Do you seriously believe global investors will continue to pull our chestnuts out of the fire by purchasing debt instruments, which they know will be repaid with money which has no basis in value other than full faith that we will print even more money?

RMM: That's what global investors do. What other kind of money do they get? You have just described the real world.

K: If the purpose of printing ever-increasing piles of paper is to satisfy unlimited societal demand, what motivation will there be to require any effort or work to produce the goods and/or services being demanded? In other words, why should I go to work on the assembly line today to produce a Cadillac . . . if I can simply express my wish for one and expect the government to print the money for it?

RMM: If the government merely gave money to everyone, there would be little need for work. With no work, nothing would be produced, and nothing would be imported.

We would have to let foreigners come into our country to produce or import goods. We would have a society similar to Saudi Arabia's.

That's a dangerous situation. The Saudis are rich in money, but economically and militarily at risk, because their citizens rely too much on non-citizens.

I do not envision most of the money, being used as gifts for the indolent. Rather, I see the government continuing to pay for goods and services, which would stimulate business. I also see the government decreasing its appetite for taxes, which again would stimulate business.

We already have come $5 trillion in that direction, and I want to continue the trend.

K: How long can such a Ponzi scheme survive?

RMM: Paper money *is* a sort of Ponzi scheme. The problem with a Ponzi scheme is it eventually runs out of money. Since the federal government can print money without limit, the scheme can continue indefinitely. It has done rather well so far. I'm sure the people of 20 years ago would have predicted disaster at the thought of a $5 trillion debt.

Our economy would collapse like a Ponzi scheme however, if the government were precluded from creating more money -- that is, a forced balancing of the budget.

October 25, 1997

S: I used to develop econometrics models for [K] Securities. Time Magazine referenced one of my papers: "Deficits and Interest Rates" in which I studied the relationship between deficits and interest rates (i.e., there is none.)

RMM: You're correct. There also is no relationship between "high" interest rates and slow GDP growth.

S: What is in your theory to support the claim that deficit spending tends to boost an economy?

RMM: The deficit spending of WWII lifted us out of the 10-year Depression. Reagan's deficit spending helped cure Carter's famous “malaise.” Further, since deficit spending is one of the factors that creates money, even the Concord people found a correlation between Total Debt and GDP growth..

S: Government does not produce anything.

RMM: Except money for roads, armies, health care, retirement, millions of jobs, medical care, education, social services, etc.

S: Government is a deadweight loss on the economy. Don't let short-term effects fool you. Deficit spending eventually takes a big toll -- debt service strangles the economy just like a person on a credit card binge.

RMM: So the bigger the debt, the more strangled we should be. Look around. The debt has grown enormously, and so has the economy. There is absolutely no mechanism for government debt service to strangle an economy. The reverse is true. Government debt service pumps money into the economy.

S: As a banker, I see this syndrome in borrowers more often than I would otherwise expect.

RMM: Differentiate between the federal government and all other borrowers. You and I can be strangled by debt. The federal government cannot. It is the one borrower that can create all the money it needs.

S: With this larger debt load, how will we keep inflation in check through 2000?

RMM: Did you ask that question during the early days of Reagan, when the debt was less than $1 trillion? Now its almost $6 trillion. Where's the inflation? How have we done it? Answer: Interest rate control.

October 28, 1997
RF: Suggests the following change in Social Security payments:
Total income including
means-tested entitlements

Percentage reduction in entitlement payments that exceed $40,000.

| | |
|---|---|
| $ 0 to $40,000 | 0% |
| $40,000 to $50,000 | 10% |
| $50,000 to $60,000 | 20% |
| $60,000 to $70,000 | 30% |
| $70,000 to $80,000 | 40% |
| $80,000 to $90,000 | 50% |
| $90,000 to $100,000 | 60% |
| $100,000 to $110,000 | 70% |
| $110,000 to $120,000 | 80% |
| $120,000 and above | 85% |

RMM: First we tax the “rich” ($120K is rich?) 36% + 7.65% FICA and another 7.65% if they own their own business. Then we take away 85% of the Social Security they paid for with those taxes. And finally, when they die, tax the money they want to leave to their heirs.

This plan doesn’t only soak the rich. It begins to punish people as soon as they make $40,000, barely survival for people in urban areas.

October 29, 1997

C: All the means-test does is eliminate the "windfall" payments for the upper brackets.

RMM: According to the Law of Unintended Consequences, it does other things.

1. It discourages working productively after 65.
2. It discourages 401k and other retirement plans, since they would be considered in a means test.
3. It encourages retired people to transfer income from their assets to their kids, plus other clever tricks, to defeat the means test.
4. It encourages establishment of a another bureaucracy to monitor the means test and to catch people who cheat.
5. It encourages the hiring of prosecutors to track down the people who cheat.
6. It encourages building jail cells to deal with those malfeasors.

While we strive for tax simplification, the last thing we need is yet another complication.

By the way, did you really intend to call it a "means" test? One can have a good income, but limited means. (What if at the age of 70, you owed ten million dollars and earned $200,000 a year? Are you in the upper brackets?)

As to Social Security's "windfall payments," you are referring to after-tax money, that was invested in an extremely poor investment no one would voluntarily make (you get nothing if you die before 65), the income from which already is taxed at inordinate rates.

I imagine if you live to 100, you come out pretty well, though, you'd have to live in poverty to satisfy the means test..

Consider an insurance annuity into which you paid all your life and received nothing if you died before 65, and didn't break even until you were in your 90's. Would you buy it?

October 29, 1997

C: People much smarter than me have thought this idea (federal surplus) through and figured out that it can work.

RMM: Smart people created the Great Depression. Smart people created the original Social Security program, and smart people created all the changes that have come since. Smart people created the current debt. The question is, whom do you follow?

October 31, 1997

K: Compare the increase in the standard of living since 1947 with the increase in federal debt and you'll find that in the first 25 years (1947-1972) we had a successive string of balanced budgets/ surpluses or very small deficits. And what happened to the standard of living during these 25 years? Answer: it doubled.

RMM: Selected data. What about the years prior to 1929, when we ran a budget surplus, which led to the Great Depression? What about 1939 - 1945, when we had a huge deficit, which finally brought us out of the Depression?

During the years 1947-1972, Total Debt increased enormously, which meant that consumers and businesses were borrowing furiously, and took the money creation burden off the federal government. Now consumers are up to their eyeballs in debt. So who is going to create the money for future expansion?

Also, that phrase, “standard of living,” has been interpreted more ways than a Casey Stengel speech. No one knows which of the thousands of economic numbers represent the “real” American standard of living. Actually, I prefer GDP and inflation as most representative.

Others may prefer “% of people below the 'poverty line'” (another imaginary number), the difference between “wealthy” and “poor” (two more imaginary numbers). Or do you like median wage, median wage for the principal breadwinner, total unemployed, total unemployed but not seeking work, median hours worked, median vacation days, median value of job-supplied benefits or median value of government supplied benefits?

How about median education, median car ownership, median age of 1st car, median home ownership, or median value of median home owned (including or not including condos)?

Or, there's median value of 2nd home and 2nd home ownership, average savings (but we don't know what "savings" are), average spending for nonessentials, average ownership of major appliances and average cost of those appliances and average entertainment expenditures.

And, don't forget average calorie intake (to demonstrate the hunger factor), average calorie intake by the lowest income quadrant.

And, what standard of living analysis would be complete without discussing health. We can consider average # of doctors per capita, average specialists (of various kinds) per capita, and there's the all-important demonstration of "standard of living": average life span.

What is the mechanism that would cause a tax increase to increase our "standard of living?" Are you saying, if we had kept raising taxes during the Depression, we wouldn't have had to wait for the wartime deficits to get us out?

October 31, 1997

K: Of all the factors that led to the Great Depression, the facts that the Federal Reserve did not lower interest rates and did not pump money into the financial system were much larger factors. The Fed allowed the money supply to shrink by one-third from late 1929 until 1932. As we know, that's the wrong reaction.

RMM: You are right.

K: Hoover pushed through the Smoot-Hawley Tariff in the spring of 1930. This action completed a 1928 campaign promise, but it resulted in a collapse of world trade and USA exports.

RMM: True. Tariffs are taxes. They destroy money.

K: Then, Andrew Mellon, in one of his last acts as Secretary of the Treasury, asked Congress to raise taxes significantly (a 55 percent rate on the richest) -- which slowed the economy still further. A contracting money supply, a horrible tariff, and tax increases. Rodger, you want to blame budget surpluses? Please!

RMM: There are only two ways to achieve Concord's budget surplus – increase taxes and spend less.

A contracting money supply? That's the definition of a budget surplus. A horrible tariff? That's taxation. And tax increases? Well, we know what they are. What the government did was exactly what Concord wants done, again.

K: The federal government ran substantial deficits from 1931-1940 without stopping the Depression. How do you account for that? How do you account for the second wave of the Depression hitting after 1936 -- after five years of large deficit spending? Under your proposal, does that make sense?

Also, the deficits of the 1930's were, for the most part, at least twice as large as the surpluses of the 1920's. How do you account for that? Shouldn't the Depression have ended in 1935 or so under your guidelines?

RMM: It's true that from 1930 to 1940, Federal debt rose from $17 billion to $54 billion. However, the key figure, Total Debt, did not rise at all. In 1930, Total Debt was $214 billion. In 1935, Total Debt had fallen to $200 billion, which accounts for the "second wave" of depression. By 1940, Total debt was only at $216 billion.

The reason we couldn't recover from the Depression is that Federal debt did not increase enough to overcome the drop in all other forms of money creation. In 1941 however, Total Debt began to rise, which ended the Depression.

It doesn't matter what kind of money is created, so long as the total supply increases significantly.

C: You are right: the Second World War ended the Great Depression. It forced full employment through the military and industrial processes. Saying federal deficits ended the Depression is incredibly disingenuous.

RMM: Wars do not force employment. Wars just kill people. There have been wars in Angola, Pakistan, India, Russia, all through Africa, Viet Nam, Korea, etc. that did not force employment in these areas.

Employment is forced by government spending. Federal deficits ended the Depression. Had there been no war, and the government spent as much, the Depression would have ended, and without all the killing.

G: Also, as you know, many of us in the Concord Coalition agree that deficit spending can be a useful economic stimulant when necessary.

RMM: Who decides when it's necessary? When is improving the economy not necessary? The poor of America think its necessary now.

What about the people, whose Social Security and Medicare are cut? Wouldn't they think stimulating the economy is necessary? Is improving our infrastructure, education, police, etc., necessary now?

C: The problem is that we have run huge deficits during good times since 1981. Now, if we need to fight a war or deal with a major economic problem, we find ourselves in a situation where we have already spent that money.

RMM: The amount of money in the world is not fixed.. Spending money doesn't destroy it.

January 24, 1998

CCC The Concord Coalition's position is that if budget surpluses occur, they should be strategically deployed to reduce the level of public debt.

RMM: To "reduce the level of public debt" means, "to reduce the amount of money in circulation."

CCC: This is more likely than any other use of surpluses to help the entire nation build a strong economy and at the same time ensure that entitlement benefits for seniors are consistent both with their needs and the ability of younger generations to finance them.

RMM: There is no mechanism by which reducing the amount of money in circulation will build a strong economy and pay entitlement benefits.

CCC: The late 1990s mark a point when the federal budget should be substantially in surplus, not barely in balance.

RMM: A federal budget "substantially in surplus" means the total amount of money in our economy would decline substantially. This will cause a depression as it has in the past.

CCC: The public debt should decline during favorable circumstances in order to allow the debt to increase when necessity arises.

RMM: This assumes there is some ceiling on what the government can borrow. I know of no such ceiling.

CCC: The fiscal climate is more favorable today than it has been for many decades or is likely to be for many decades to come.

RMM: This favorable fiscal climate has come during one of the largest run-ups in federal debt in our history.

CCC: Generational equity requires some correspondence between how much a generation pays to government and how much it gets back in return.

RMM: Running a surplus means that *everyone* pays to the government more than they get back.

CCC: Simple generational fairness to our kids requires today's workers and owners of capital to build budget surpluses today to pay for their own retirement and health insurance benefits tomorrow.

RMM: "Generational fairness?" Is this related to "tax fairness" which means whatever the speaker wants, and therefore impossible to achieve.

Every political act in history has been done in the name of "fairness," from Hitler's "living space," to Marx's communism, from the New Deal to the Great Society, from school busing to "separate but equal," from racial preferences to equality.

In Chicago we have the debate between those who want to promote police on the basis of test scores vs. those who want "merit promotions." Both espouse fairness.

CCC: Budget surpluses by definition increase national savings and free funds for investments that will increase productivity and raise economic growth rates.

RMM: If the government raises your taxes and/or spends less in our economy (the two mechanisms for creating a surplus), how will this "free funds for investments?" If I pay more taxes, and/or my business receives less money from the government, how does that free my funds for investment?

January 25, 1998

MP: You suggest that because the ratio of workers to retirees has declined in the past without creating serious problems, future declines can also occur problem-free. In a pay-as-you-go system, such as ours, where workers' payroll taxes (as well as general revenues, for that matter) provide the wherewithal to pay for retirees' Social Security and Medicare benefits, the scale of how many workers there are for every retiree does indeed matter.

RMM: Workers' payroll taxes do not pay for SS or Medicare. All taxes – income, FICA and Medicare – go into one big pot. When there isn't enough in the pot, the government borrows.

It makes no more sense to call SS and Medicare "pay-as-you-go" than it does to call payments for defense, infrastructure, education, housing, food stamps or any of the other thousands of government programs "pay-as-you-go."

Nothing has been pay-as-you-go for many years. That's one reason why the government has debt. (The other reason is: if the government didn't have debt, there would be no government money in existence.)

MP: What if there were eight or six retirees for every worker? Don't you think this would be a problem? How about three retirees or two for every worker? Extreme examples but they make the point.

RMM: Not extreme at all. There would be no problem if there were a hundred retirees for every worker.

MP: There would be no way that workers could comfortably fork over enough tax dollars to support benefits for this many retirees and still have enough to raise their own families and meet their own needs.

RMM: Correct, there is no way. So why try to do it? The ratio of workers to retirees will continue falling, so any tax-based solution will be temporary, and meanwhile, will hurt the workers.

January 30, 1998

MP: Without investments in tools, research and development, communications and transportation infrastructure, education and training, we will not be able to continue to increase the output per unit of work.

RMM: True.

MP: And, of course, to make investments, there must be resources (usually money).

RMM: Absolutely true.

MP: And to come up with the resources, people must save rather than consume.

RMM: Absolutely true -- or absolutely false -- depending on what you define as saving and what you define as consuming. A common form of saving is the purchase of T-bills, which Concord wants to reduce.

On the other hand, you probably consider the purchase of a home PC to be a form of consumption. Yet it provides computer manufacturers with the resources to conduct research and develop new methods and products. If not for that "consumption," we wouldn't see the amazing advances in computer technology.

January 31, 1998:

MP: I agree it is very hard to know what investments will yield how much increase in productivity. But as we look ahead to a labor force that will almost stop growing, if we want to see continuing increases in our economic well being, we will have to increase our efforts to boost productivity.

RMM: Private investors do not consider what is best for the country, but rather, what investment will yield the best return. They already invest as well as they can. Therefore, private investment will not "increase its efforts" to boost productivity.

Only government has the means to expend money and energy to improve the overall good of the nation, without expecting a dollar return.

Any "increase in efforts" must come from government, not from the private sector. Government can "increase its efforts" in two ways: by offering incentives (usually tax incentives) or by spending directly. When the government wanted more returning soldiers to go to college, it instituted the G.I. Bill, which paid for hundreds of thousands of ex-G.I.s to get schooling. Private industry would not and could not have accomplished this.

When the government wanted to foster the American Dream of owning a house, it provided tax incentives to individuals and to the real estate industry.

Note that both the G. I. Bill and tax incentives lead to deficits, not surpluses. The only way to "increase our efforts," is for the government to run deficits.

February 6, 1998

RD: As best as I can gather, you believe there is no limit to the debt at any point in time.

RMM: I had a pleasant phone conversation with a member of this list who said, "There must be some limit to the amount of debt the government safely can issue." I had to agree. There must be some limit.

Everything has a limit, even the universe. However, Concordians use the "there-must-be-some-limit" argument to say, "therefore, let's balance the budget."

The notion that there may be a limit doesn't logically mean we have reached that limit. When the man asked me what I thought the limit was, I said, "At least $36 trillion within the next 18 years." Where did I get that figure? The debt has grown 6-fold in the past 18 years and the economy is doing well.

Based on that test, another 6-fold increase would seem to be the minimum level of safe increase.

RD: I have never heard you admit that debt can be negative. This saves you from having to judge where the limit might lie or that types of debt may have what types of negative effects.

RMM: Debt can be negative if you are the debtor, and you don't have the unlimited ability to create money to service the debt. That includes every entity except the federal government.

RD: You say that balanced budgets/ paying down the debt contracts the money supply, and that an expanding money supply is an essential precursor, catalyst, or key ingredient for economic growth. But, unless I've missed it, I've seen little discussion by you about the role of productivity rate growth and/or investment as they relate to economic growth or increasing the money supply.

RMM: One thing I feel certain about: Decreasing the money supply will not help productivity or investment or economic growth. Certain kinds of investments do increase the money supply, specifically investments in debt.

February 10, 1998

BA: If interests rates do not affect economic growth, then why does the Fed lower rates when the economy is headed for recession and raise rates if economic growth is thought to be too high and will result in inflation?

Obviously there is a lag in the effects of rate changes; rates are raised when the economy is booming and later the economy slows. Conversely, when the economy is slowing, rates are lowered and later the economy improves.

However, interest rates are only one of many factors that affect the economy. Reagan significantly lowered the tax rates that resulted in more money in the private sector, which tends to use that money more efficiently than the government.

RMM: If you saying that tax decreases help the economy by adding money to the economy, I agree.

BA: Assume the government borrows $100,000 to pay 10 people on welfare a $10,000 a year annual benefit. These people spend the money on food, etc. but produce no additional goods or services to spur the economy.

RMM: The money spent on food, etc. goes to the businesses that sell food -- canners, freezers, packers -- who produce "additional goods and services."

Then it goes to the farmers and fishermen, who spend it on tractors, plows and barns. From there it goes to other businesses, all of which produce "additional goods or services to spur the economy." Money doesn't stop with its first use. All money is equally beneficial to the U.S. as it travels through the economy.

BA: Not many got upset with government debt, as Reagan expanded the military and the Democratic Congress expanded the welfare state. However, many became concerned when the federal government seemed to be getting out of control with an ever accelerating rate of spending.

RMM: Actually, government debt is the most "in-control" money creation we have. Congress has the power to determine it to the last dollar. Congress has little control over private debt creation, and that is why we cannot depend on private debt to support the nation if federal debt declines.

BA: There needs to be a balance between the private sector and the government sector in not only debt, but in the control of our lives!

RMM: Federal debt as a percentage of Total Debt has declined. So what balance do you like? 50/50? 70/30? 80/20? Which of these ratios is superior to any other?

Speaking of federal control over our lives, people have been concerned about big business controlling our lives, and demanded that the government do something about it. Standard Oil, AT&T, Microsoft, to name a few.

February 16, 1998

RD: I do not see the obvious lack of any relationship (between interest rates and GDP growth) that you claimed to see. The uncorrected GDP seems to generally trend up until 1977 and then down while the discount rate seems to trend up until 1982 and then down.

However, the short term ups and downs still tend to move in opposite directions for interest rates and the GDP. I have never claimed to have proven that there is a relationship. But I think the graph definitely showed that your claims of showing no relationship are totally unfounded.

RMM: When I look at the 40-year period 1957-1997, I see the discount rate ranging from about 3% to about 14%, and the median at about 6%. During the same period, the annual % change in GDP is about 7%.

The discount rate was below 6% 23 times. During that same time span, the GDP % increase was below 7% 23 times. If interest rates have an adverse effect on GDP % increase, you should expect that the low GDP % increases should occur at times of high interest rates.

Exactly the opposite occurs. The vast majority of low GDP % increases occur in years that had the low interest rates. The vast majority of high GDP increases occur in years that had the higher interest rates.

You considered a 3% interest rate as "high" if the previous year were only 2%. And you considered an 11% rate as "low" if the previous year were 14%. I disagree. If interest rates decline from 14% to 11%, they're still high and, if common wisdom were correct, should correspond with low GDP growth.

But higher interest rates corresponded with high GDP growth, and certainly did not contribute to low GDP growth.

February 28, 1998

BB: There are two major problems with polls. First, the way the questions are worded and asked can have a major impact on the results. . . . Unless the press assures that the public gets truthful information, it will be difficult for Congress to pass effective legislation on SS and tax reform.

RMM: Words such as "reform" and "deficit" are among the most misleading words. "Reform" simply means "change" (re-form), but it has such a positive cachet, virtually everyone favors reform, no matter what the subject. If you ask, "Are you in favor of tax reform," a majority will answer, "Yes," despite lack of knowledge regarding the form the "reform" would take.

"Deficit" is used to describe the situation in which the economy receives more money from the government than the economy sends to the government -- in other words, an economic surplus. However the word "deficit" has such a negative cachet, virtually everyone is opposed to any type of "deficit."

If you ask, "Do you want to see our economy run a deficit," (a federal government budget surplus), a majority will say, "No."

March 2, 1998

RMM: Today's Chicago Tribune included an article saying that budget considerations soon will force us to decide who should receive dialysis and who should die the painful, nausea-ridden death of acute kidney failure.

The author seemed to lean toward two solutions: (1) An age limit, whereby people older than 55 (!) would be refused treatment, and/or (2) A financial test whereby people "who could afford it" would be required to pay for this treatment.

Solution (1) is not worthy of consideration, since it arbitrarily condemns people to death, when lifesaving treatment is available. Most Americans would find this solution repugnant.

Solution (2) likely would find adherents among some, for there seems some belief that elderly people are rich. Yet, dialysis is so expensive as to impoverish all but the wealthiest. Further, it would force families to make decisions resembling solution (1) -- that is shall I condemn my family to debt, or shall I allow my mother to die?

Finally, solution (2) would require yet another intrusive and expensive bureaucracy to determine who would be driven into abject poverty and who would merely be injured financially by having to pay.

So the budget-balancers face yet another human reality. Shall we run a federal surplus (an economic deficit), which never in our history has proven necessary or even beneficial, and force thousands of people to decide between financial ruin and death?

Or shall we continue to allow the government to create money, which history shows has benefitted the economy as well as the health and longevity of our people?

Place a human face on the economic deficit (a.k.a. federal surplus), and it looks quite unattractive.

Mon, 23 Mar 1998 09:31:50
You have been removed from the CONCORD-L list (The Concord Coalition Discussion List) by Craig Cheslog <ccheslog@EROLS.COM>.

Sadly, nothing has changed. As recently as 2/1/01 Ellie Fink, of the Concord Coalition wrote:

Dear Mr. Mitchell: The money to grow the economy comes from private savings. When government debt is paid down, private savings is freed up for investment in training, plant, and equipment. More investment means more jobs and a growing economy. Government investment -- in education and infrastructure, for example -- is an investment in the country's future that makes the economy and the country stronger, too.
Sincerely, Ellanor S. Fink, Member Relations, The Concord Coalition

2/6/01:
RMM: Thanks for your response, Ellanor: Paying down government debt requires taxes to increase and/or government spending to decrease. In a surplus, the economy sends more money to the government (taxes) than the government returns to the economy (spending). Therefore, paying down the debt removes money from the economy.

How do increased taxes free up private saving?

How does a reduction in government spending increase government investment?

How does removing money from the economy help the economy grow?

Rodger Malcolm Mitchell

## Other Mail

To: *The Economist Magazine* from Rodger Mitchell, 2/15/99: When discussing additional loans to Russia, your Feb 6th editorial says, " . . . any further western money is likely to be squandered." This is the classic "first use" misunderstanding.

Once money enters an economy it circulates endlessly, spent repeatedly on worthwhile and not-so-worthwhile projects. If the first use of money lent to Russia would be "squandered" into politicians' pockets, what would the politicians do with it?

Spend it on food, aiding food store owners and then farmers and farm suppliers? Or would they buy clothing, aiding retailers and clothing manufacturers and button makers? . Or would the money be put in the politicians' banks, allowing the banks to lend and create more money, enriching the entire society?

After its "first use," all money is equal and will continue to do good for an economy until it is destroyed by taxation.

For an economy, it is not possible for money to be "squandered." It only can be created or destroyed.

A growing economy requires a growing supply of money. Where will Russia find this growing supply? From the same source the U.S. has used. We created $6 trillion in debt (money), fueling our successful economy. Russia must create much more debt by printing money, while protecting the value of this debt through interest rate control.

Russia should use newly-minted roubles to buy dollars and to service its external debt. Would you trade dollars for roubles if you could get a 20% return in dollars? Would you do it for 50%? 1,000%? At some level of interest, your answer will be "Yes."

Does endlessly creating debt build an economy? During the years immediately preceding the Great Depression, the U.S. government ran surpluses (destroyed money). The country began to emerge from the depression, only when the government borrowed heavily (created lots of money) to finance WWII. Reagan's massive money creation set the stage for our current boom.

In short, Russia should print roubles, raise interest rates, buy dollars and service its debts.

Rodger Malcolm Mitchell, Wilmette, IL

From: Edward Lucas, Moscow Bureau Chief, The Economist, Subject: Fwd.: How Russia Can Save Itself; Date: Tue., 16 Feb. 1999 14:46:28: Thanks for your letter. It is important not to overlook that Russia is a very open economy. In the past, money lent has gone to offshore bank accounts very quickly (any roubles created have had a negligible effect because of the corrupt banking system).

Printing roubles and raising interest rates as you describe would lead to a hyper-inflationary crash which would make our current problems seem like a picnic. Don't forget the horrible effects of high interest rates on the economy (especially in late payments of wages and other bills)

Regards, Edward Lucas

To Edward Lucas:

You expressed legitimate concern about increasing the supply of roubles as inflationary. Yet, to grow, an economy absolutely requires an increased supply of money.

Question: Given every economy's need to increase the supply of money, how does one accomplish that without inflation?

Answer: Money is a commodity, the value of which is determined by supply and demand. Increase the supply and indeed you will have inflation . . . unless you also increase demand.

What determines the demand for money? Risk and reward. Reward means interest on government issued debt. Risk means the likelihood of debt default and/or inflation. Thus, raising interest rates prevents or cures inflation, depending on whether inflation already exists, by increasing demand.

Contrary to common belief and short-term stock market movements, high interest rates do not adversely affect an economy. For every interest payer there is an interest earner. The interest money circulates within the economy, neither enriching it nor impoverishing it over time. I

If high interest rates are combined with an increase in the supply of money, the economy will be stimulated without inflation. Consumers, having more money, will spend more and business will earn more; there will be no late payments of salaries, because there will be no inflationary motive for delay.

You also expressed concern about deposits in "offshore bank accounts," which presumably would decrease the domestic supply of money. Thus you have expressed concern about both increasing and decreasing the supply of money. I do not know which category "corrupt banking system" would fall into.

Depositing money in a bank creates money, for banks always use money as the basis for loans. In America, $1 deposited in a bank, creates $10 of new money, the effect of which is identical to the government printing $10 of new money. (Those who advocate increased bank savings while deploring increased printing of money, are taking opposite sides of the same question -- sometimes called "cognitive dissonance," the ability to believe opposite positions simultaneously.)

Again, thank you for your comments, Rodger Malcolm Mitchell

. . . . . . . . . . . . . . . . . . . . . . . . . . . . . . . . . . . . . . . . . . . . . . . . .

To: Terry Savage, Business Columnist for the *Chicago Sun Times*
April 11, 1999

Hi, Terry. When last we spoke, you were leaving for travel, and I hope had a pleasant trip. Perhaps you will find this thought-provoking:

There seems widespread belief that once a dollar is spent it ceases forever to exist in our economy. How else can you explain this headline on your competitor's business page (Saturday, April 10, 1999)?: "Judge awards S&L $909 million -- Precedent could cost taxpayer $50 billion more." The writer, Stephen Labaton of the New York Times News Service, goes on to say, "The huge bailout of the savings and loan industry . . . has already cost taxpayers $165 billion and administration officials estimate that every $1 billion in judgments will cost each American household $10."

Labaton seems to believe that when the government spends $50 billion, this money instantly disappears, the result being a net loss to taxpayers. Yet where has this $165 billion "cost" to the taxpayers gone? Labaton answers the question: "Prominent businessmen who hold big stakes in savings associations" and "thousands of smaller investors."

Who are these businessmen and investors if not taxpayers? The $165 billion that came from taxpayers, went to taxpayers. The money merely recirculated.

What Labaton refers to as "the most expensive financial debacle in American history," merely was a massive recirculation of money. It didn't cost the taxpayers a dime.

In truth, the most expensive financial debacle in American history is a federal surplus. By definition, "surplus" means the federal government takes in more tax money than it sends back into the pockets of taxpayers. While the S&L bailout cost taxpayers nothing, the surplus will cost taxpayers many billions -- just as a federal surplus did during the years immediately preceding the 1929 depression.

Rodger Malcolm Mitchell

April 21, 1999

To: Rodger Malcolm Mitchell

From: Terry Savage

Sure, Roger. The money came FROM some taxpayers, and went TO other taxpayers. I'd rather decide where my money is going TO, than letting Uncle Sam re-route it! Terry Savage

April 22, 1999

To: Terry Savage

From: Rodger Malcolm Mitchell

Me too, Terry. Yet, the point remains: The bailout of the S&Ls didn't cost taxpayers a dime. Government spending does not cost taxpayers money. Social Security, Medicare, welfare, infrastructure, housing, the police and the courts, etc. -- all are recirculations of money.

Some individuals benefit; others lose. (If you and I live long enough, we will benefit big-time). But as a group, taxpayers break even.

Media people inadvertently have misled the public, and you would do your readers a service by revealing these widely misunderstood points.

By the way, you say would rather decide where your money is going rather than letting Uncle Sam re-route it. There is only one way. Cut taxes.

Kindest regards, Rodger Malcolm Mitchell

April 24, 1999

From: Terry Savage:

Roger, I don't have time to get into a long debate, but don't be an old Keynesian, who really believes that all the govt. has to do is spend less in good times, and more in bad times. The real problem with deficits happens when the govt. monetizes the debt -- creates new money via the Fed which purchases the debt and pays for it with newly created reserves == which cheapens the value of all we have worked and saved for.

Aside from that, if I want to redistribute the money I've worked for I don't need the government to decide who it should go to! Terry

April 25, 1999

To: Terry Savage:

Terry, you said, "The real problem with deficits happens when the government monetizes the debt . . ." The word "monetize" means to turn into money. The vast majority of the debt is in the form of short term (less than one year) liabilities, like T-bills. These liabilities already are considered money ("L") by the government. It is impossible to monetize money.

Green paper can be monetized. But federal debt already is money and cannot be monetized.

You also said, ". . . the Fed purchases the debt and pays for it with newly created reserves -- which cheapens the value of all we have worked and saved for." By "cheapens the value," you mean inflation. From the Reagan administration until today, the debt has risen a remarkable 6-fold, from less than $1 trillion to $6 trillion. This is the largest debt increase in America's history.

According to the "cheapens-the-value" theory, we should have had significant inflation. Yet we have not. Conversely, we've had inflation when federal debt has risen slowly or not at all.

Kindest regards, Rodger

## *The Author by The Author*

I was born March 25, 1935 and one of my earliest memories is December 7, 1941, Pearl Harbor day. That information is appropriate only because the date marks the beginning of America's rise from a second-tier power to its current super-power status.

Twenty four hours before marrying Phyllis Rae Garber on June 17, 1956, I graduated from the University of Illinois (Champaign, IL), receiving a Bachelor of Science degree in Marketing. Six years later I received a Master of Business Administration from Northwestern University (Evanston, IL).

After college I joined Booth Fisheries, Inc., the largest frozen seafood company in America. Booth had fallen into receivership during the Great Depression, and the man assigned to run the company had been appointed by the bank, which in part explains what later happened to Booth.

As the Advertising Manager and the Purchasing Manager, I learned some of the most valuable business lessons of my life. In short, I learned how money can cause illogic.

This huge company had hired an inexperienced, twenty-one-year-old boy (me) to run their advertising, a result of their belief that advertising does not work. Booth's systems were chaotic, with most decisions being made by the President, the Sales Manager or no one.

The company did not seek the personnel needed for growth. (I remember Booth's oldest telephone salesman, who sat *under* his desk to make phone calls, because he did not want the other salesmen to hear what he said. Booth's management did not consider this strange.)

Booth's lack of systems and structure gave me access to every corner of the company, and I took advantage of this to learn the bad and even some good about the advertising, marketing, purchasing, production, sales, systems, personnel and goals of a large corporation. In business, learning what not to do sometimes can provide the most valuable lessons.

After Booth, I moved to Arthur Meyerhoff Associates, Inc., the primary advertising agency for the Wm. Wrigley, Jr. Company, the world's largest manufacturer of chewing gum.

Mr. Meyerhoff, had the ability to irritate his employees by continually telling us we were wrong. He usually was right. Meyerhoff understood money. He was pragmatic about it. He knew that to earn it, he must focus on a single corporate goal: to please his clients.

The rest of the agency personnel wanted to create the best advertising, but Mr. Meyerhoff knew that was irrelevant to the survival and prosperity of AMAI. He once said, “If the fat lady wants the bright red dress, sell her the bright red dress. You'll get no thanks for pushing her toward the more attractive black dress.” That was the reality I learned, cynical but practical.

I spent ten years as AMAI's V.P. and Management Supervisor on the Wrigley's account, which together with my Booth Fisheries education, gave me an inside look at the truths and peculiarities of corporations and of money. It was from those experiences that I developed an understanding of financial reality.

In 1980, I became a part owner of Murlas Commodities, Inc., a dying commodities futures brokerage, that had one broker and two “starving” owners. I took over operations and within a few months I had turned the brokerage around, and made it quite profitable.

In 1989 I turned to another dying company, National Law Resources. This tiny, used-law-book dealer was, if anything, in worse shape than Murlas had been. It was deeply in debt to suppliers, lenders and the IRS.

I again took over operations, and again turned the company around. It grew quickly. When I sold my share of the company, National Law Resource was doing more than half of all the used law book business in America.

In 1997, I began to help a small, troubled company named Management Simulations, Inc. As this is written, we have grown to become the world's largest supplier of business simulations to colleges and universities, as well as to such corporations as GE, GM, Allstate, PricewaterhouseCoopers, Sempra, Caterpillar, Honeywell, John Deere and many others.

I have written a book of short stories, two of which won prizes in *Writers Digest Magazine* contests. I also have written a book about building a company, titled *Getting Rich is the Sweetest Revenge.*

I wrote *FREE MONEY,* because I believe the country has an opportunity to solve its money problems, but instead was making the most terrible mistake of its economic life -- the federal surplus.

My hope is that you will see the same dangers and opportunities I do, and will contact your friends, relatives and especially your representatives in Congress, to help them see, too. If enough of us understand the problems and the solutions, our precious country may be saved and a successful future assured.

To the government, money is free. Our government can create it without limit, and give it any value we wish. We will prosper when we free money from the cognitive dissonance that binds it to the past.

***A growing economy must have a growing supply of money.***

***The federal government is the only U.S. entity that can create an unlimited amount of money.***

***Therefore, the federal government can and should end its borrowing and taxing, and very simply, create the money needed to grow our economy.***

## Index